D1207671

OXFORD LIBRARY OF AFRICAN LITERATURE

General Editors

E. E. EVANS-PRITCHARD

G. LIENHARDT

W. H. WHITELEY

Oxford Library of African Literature

A SELECTION OF AFRICAN PROSE

I. Traditional Oral Texts
II. Written Prose

Compiled by W. H. WHITELEY

(*Two volumes*)

(*not for sale in the U.S.A. or Canada*)

THE HEROIC RECITATIONS OF THE BAHIMA OF ANKOLE

By H. F. MORRIS

SOMALI POETRY

An Introduction

By B. W. ANDRZEJEWSKI *and* I. M. LEWIS

SOMALI POETRY

An Introduction

B. W. ANDRZEJEWSKI

AND

I. M. LEWIS

OXFORD

AT THE CLARENDON PRESS

1964

Oxford University Press, Amen House, London E.C.4

GLASGOW NEW YORK TORONTO MELBOURNE WELLINGTON
BOMBAY CALCUTTA MADRAS KARACHI LAHORE DACCA
CAPE TOWN SALISBURY NAIROBI IBADAN ACCRA
KUALA LUMPUR HONG KONG

PRINTED IN GREAT BRITAIN

PREFACE

This book endeavours to give the English reader some conception of the richness of Somali poetry. It is an introduction to a very extensive oral literature and we have tried to make it, within the limits of our knowledge, as representative as possible both in range of type and style of verse and song, and in quality. In applying the last criterion we have been guided by the evaluations made by contemporary Somali and have followed the canons of what we take to be accepted opinion.

We have been fortunate in being able to include a selection of the poems of Sheikh Maḥammed ʿAbdille Ḥasan, which like the other examples in our collection, have not, so far as we know, been previously translated into a European language. Apart from their poetic interest, these poems are especially valuable in throwing new light upon the character, aims, and methods, of this great Somali leader who between 1900 and 1920 unremittingly waged war against the foreign colonizers of his country and who is today regarded as one of the founders of Somali nationalism. We have been at pains also to include in our collection a number of religious poems which illuminate the Muslim basis of Somali life. Unlike the other poems in this collection these are not only orally recorded but are also preserved in Arabic; an Arabic, we may add, which as the Arabist will see contains some local colloquialisms and sometimes words of Somali origin. The inclusion of these religious poems will serve, we hope, to give a more rounded, and a more true impression of Somali life and culture.

Yet, despite these aims, we cannot of course claim that our volume is fully comprehensive. The Somali reader, particularly, will join us in regretting the omission of works by such well-known poets as ʿAbdi Gahayr, Qawḍan Duʿaale, Qamaan Bulḥaan, ʿAli Ḍuuḥ, and Gabay-Shinni; and no doubt other names which should have been included will suggest themselves to the critical reader. Perhaps, however, these shortcomings may be forgiven if, as we hope, they encourage others to fill the gaps left in our collection.

In collecting our material, and in obtaining the commentaries upon each poem which are so essential if its meaning is to be understood, we have been very fortunate in being able to call upon the friendly advice and guidance of a fairly large circle of expert Somali opinion. Our greatest debt, other than to our authors, is to such well-known authorities on Somali literature and language as Mr. Musa Galaal of the Ministry of Education, Somali Republic; Mr. Yusuf Maygag Sammatar of the Ministry of Information; Mr. Abdi Salan Sayyid Suleman, the well-known broadcaster; and Mr. Shirreh Jama whose ingenious orthography we have adopted. Without their help in the translation and collation of the texts, and in the case of Mr. Musa Galaal particularly in the actual collection of some of the material, our work would have been seriously handicapped. We must also mention Sheikh Jama Umar Ise, who, for the past six years, has been engaged in an intensive study of the history and poetry of Sayyid Maḥammed ʿAbdille Ḥasan. Sheikh Jama has been kind enough to advise us on the most authentic versions of some of Maḥammed ʿAbdille Ḥasan's poems in our collection. In the case of our Arabic material we have also benefited by being able to consult Dr. J. S. Trimingham. Finally, we must thank Mrs. Sheila Andrzejewski and Mrs. C. McCulloch for their typing and other secretarial assistance.

It is trite to remark that the translation of poetry from one culture and language into another is extremely difficult. But we should be failing in our duty to the reader if we did not indicate some of the special difficulties which occur in translating from the predominantly oral literature of the Somali. Sometimes we have had to decide, on the basis of expert Somali advice, between different versions of the same poem, or of parts of a poem, and while we think that the versions we present are those generally accepted we cannot rule out the possibility of other acceptable versions. In translation itself one of the greatest difficulties, especially in serious Somali poetry, is that much of the poets' language is not that of ordinary speech today. In addition, words are often used in several widely different senses, so that ambiguity is common; and while we think that our renderings convey the main sense of the poems in our selection, we cannot always be certain that other translations might not be equally valid. Those who know Somali well, of course, will be able to judge for themselves from the texts which accompany the translations.

The position is further complicated by the freedom with which Somali poets invent new words and coin expressions to suit the alliteration and style of their verse. This idiosyncratic quality of Somali poetry poses formidable problems for the translator, and here we have to rely on our understanding of the cultural background and particular context of a poem, as well as upon what we know of the poet's special style and vocabulary. It is hardly necessary to add that we should not have been able to get very far, or to have offered our renderings with much confidence, without again relying heavily upon the advice of Somali authorities.

In our translations we have tried to adhere as closely as possible to the original texts. We have thus aimed at almost literal translation without endeavouring to reproduce the alliterative style of a poem, while seeking to convey, as accurately as possible, its imagery in its own terms. We hope that against our short account of the social and cultural background of Somali poetry our translations are fully, and readily intelligible. And we trust that at least our collection may serve to indicate something of the truly remarkable riches of the Somali poetic heritage. We hope also that those who know the country and its people may gain from this selection of poetry a new and deeper insight into Somali culture and modes of thought.

Our transcription of Somali and Arabic names in the English parts of this book follows standard practice, except that we have indicated long vowels by doubling, e.g., *aa*, instead of with a macron, *ā*. Since there is as yet no official orthography for Somali, in the transcription of our texts we have followed that devised by Mr. Shirreh Jama. This differs from the preceding only in the use of *dh* for *ḍ*; *ch* for *ḥ*; and *c* for ʿ (ain). The problems of Somali orthography are discussed further below (pp. 38–41).

Finally, we should point out that while one of us is a linguist and the other a social anthropologist, our translations, like our book as a whole, are the outcome of collaboration at every stage. Thus we jointly accept responsibility for our renderings, and trust that such success as this book may have will stimulate other linguists and anthropologists, specializing in a common area, to engage in similar co-operative ventures. Our experience, certainly, is that such collaboration is mutually beneficial; and perhaps the best measure of dependence in this case is that neither of us alone would readily have undertaken to prepare this volume.

B. W. A.
I. M. L.

CONTENTS

PART ONE

INTRODUCTION

A · THE SOCIAL AND CULTURAL SETTING

I · INTRODUCTORY

It is perhaps not too much to claim that the Somali are a nation of bards: and their poetry certainly is one of their principal cultural achievements. Poetry occupies a large and important place in Somali culture, interest in it is universal, and skill in it something which everyone covets and many possess. The Somali poetic heritage is a living force intimately connected with the vicissitudes of everyday life.

But to understand the place poetry occupies in their life and culture and to gain something more than a merely cursory appreciation of its content and allusions, it is necessary to have some idea of the material and social conditions in which it has its roots and from which it draws its inspiration. This is important not because Somali poetry is full of esoteric imagery, or concerned largely with the exotic symbolism of strange rites and ceremonies—it is neither of these things—but mainly because of the difficulties of conveying adequately in translation the flavour and allusions of a pastoral life such as that followed by the Somali. Clearly their values and aspirations are not those of many who may read this selection of their poetry. And to savour and appreciate what is said in their poetry it is necessary to set their verse in its cultural context. Moreover, the foreign reader should be better enabled to judge the kind and the quality of their poetic themes and imagery when he knows something of the world in which it is composed.

Nor is it merely that Somali values and culture illuminate their poetry. Their verse reveals the way in which their poets see their world. And something of the true significance of poetry, in their culture generally, can be judged when it is realized that not even a superficial account of Somali society and culture would be complete without some mention of the role and character of their poetry.

For while some poems commemorate events in the private life of the poet, few events in Somaliland are really private; most have a social dimension. Much of Somali verse, indeed, is composed directly in relation to a social situation, and is designed to influence the opinion, either of a body of kinsmen or of the public at large. Thus some of the longer serious poems incite kinsmen to avenge past wrongs, others to forget them; and praise and blame are most effectively spread about the country through this medium. For memorable verse spreads rapidly and is not easily forgotten. Serious poetry, indeed, is closely allied to oratory, another art which the Somali esteem highly and in which many clansmen excel.

Thus poetry is frequently employed to publicize events and as propaganda for or against some person, group, or matter of concern. Good poetry fulfills this role of broadcasting information as effectively as the press or radio in other countries, especially in a country where, although few can read, news travels with amazing rapidity. This is especially true of such noble lines as those employed by Sheikh Maḥammed 'Abdille Ḥasan[1] in his poetic diatribes against his enemies. Yet truly memorable verse persists for generations, long after the original situation in which it was composed has passed, and in many cases is known throughout the length and breadth of the Somali peninsula—from the Gulf of Aden to the Northern Province of Kenya. Such poetry is remembered for its power and for the quality of its imagery and style. Sometimes too a further occasion occurs when a particular poem can again be used for much the same purpose as that for which it was composed. This is true, for example, of the poem 'The Death of Richard Corfield' (pp. 70–74).

Although there is no special class of fully professional poets in Somaliland, because of the social importance of poetry, skill in versification is a valuable component in prestige and arms a gifted poet sometimes more effectively than weapons or wealth. Thus it is not without significance that Sheikh Maḥammed 'Abdille Ḥasan (known to an earlier generation in England as 'The Mad Mullah'), who led the rebellion against the foreign colonizers between 1900 and 1920 which we describe below, was by general consent one of the greatest of recent Somali poets. His verse, a selection of which forms the core of this book, and the memory of his struggle are still very much alive today.

[1] See below, p. 12 and pp. 53–56. The names Maḥammed and 'Abdille are Somali equivalents of Arabic Muḥammad and 'Abdulla.

II · THE PEOPLE AND THEIR DISTRIBUTION

The Somali, who, like their neighbours in North East Africa—the Danakil, Saho, and Galla—belong to the Hamitic (or Cushitic) ethnic group, number between three and three-and-a-half million persons, and occupy a large continuous tract of territory. Their country, the Somali peninsula, stretches from French Somaliland in the north, where half the population (about 29,000) are Somali, to the northern part of Kenya where they make up over half the provincial population (200,000). Their greatest strength is in the Somali Republic (including the former British Somaliland Protectorate) where they probably number almost two and a half millions. A large community of Somali (perhaps three quarters of a million) also live in the contiguous Harar and Sidamo Provinces of Ethiopia. Smaller numbers of Somali have penetrated, mainly as traders, into many of the towns of East Africa, into Aden, where there is a substantial Somali settlement, the ports of the Persian Gulf, and some of the principal American and European ports, where Somali seamen have established small fluctuating immigrant communities.

In their physical features Somali are usually tall, their heads long and narrow in shape, and their skin colour varying from light brown with a reddish tinge to dark black. Their features often also betray their Arabian connexion; and in the south of the Somali Republic, amongst the Digil and Rahanwiin Somali, there is physical evidence of their former relations with the non-Hamitic Bantu or negroid peoples, with whom many Somali clans mingled when they entered this region several centuries ago.

Although Somali are intensely conscious of their own independent nationhood, they also traditionally prize their Arabian ancestry; and this is in keeping with their strong adherence to the Muslim faith. Indeed ultimately, although among the modern élite it is no longer so fashionable to do so as it once was, Somali delight in tracing their pedigrees back to Arabian origins, and generally claim some connexion with the lineage of the Prophet himself. And despite the fact that often these claims appear to be without sound historical foundation, they are important in providing a validation for the firmly Muslim basis of Somali life and culture. They also reflect the connexion over many centuries in trade and settlement between the Somali peninsula and Arabia; a link to which the Somali owe their conversion to Islam.

As a whole, the Somali nation can conveniently be divided into two great divisions: the Northern Somali and the Southern Somali. The former comprise four large groups of clans, or 'clan-families': the Dir, Isaaq, Daarood, and Hawiye; the latter, two clan-families: the Digil and Rahanwiin. The Southern Somali, so defined, are largely cultivators living in the relatively fertile zone between the Shebelle and Juba Rivers in the south of the Somali Republic. The Northern Somali, who are concentrated mainly in the arid lands to the north of the Shebelle, are primarily pastoral nomads. Some members of this division, however, extend beyond and to the south of the Juba River, by-passing the Digil and Rahanwiin, and stretching into Kenya where they form the dominant Somali element in the population.

This distribution, which has brought Northern Somali to the most southerly limits of Somali extension, is the result of a long series of migratory movements from the Gulf of Aden littoral over the last ten centuries. In the course of these, of which more will be said later, earlier Bạntu and Galla communities (the latter predominating) were displaced or partly absorbed by conquering Somali. Those Somali who settled in the arable regions between the Shebelle and Juba Rivers—the only two substantial permanent water-courses in the entire area—adopted cultivation and mingled with a number of Galla. This led to the formation of the agricultural Digil and Rahanwiin Somali with their own distinctive habits, culture, and dialect,[1] and with a more hierarchical political organization, based on territorial interests, than that of their northern pastoral kinsmen. The further movement of northern pastoral nomads into Kenya, largely at the expense of further Galla settlers, took place in the main as recently as the late nineteenth and early twentieth centuries. It was only effectively arrested by the establishment of administrative posts about 1912.

Although the Southern Somali are not lacking in poetic skill, it is particularly the Northern Somali who have developed this

[1] On Somali dialects see below, pp. 37–38.

side of Somali oral literature so notably. It is consequently with the poetry of the northern nomads, rather than with that of the southern cultivators that this book is concerned. All the poems and songs in our collection are in Northern Somali dialects. In what follows, therefore, we shall be dealing with the northern nomads and their pastoral existence, although some further references must be made to the history of the south.

III · HISTORICAL FACTORS

1. *Settlement and Migration Prior to European Intervention*

Before proceeding farther with this short sketch of Somali culture and society, a little more must be said of Somali history. In this context it is important to realize that despite the fact that their cultural nationalism has a long tradition, it is only recently, since colonization and independence, that this has been translated, and not yet fully, into political nationhood. In the past the Somali have never formed a single political entity and have existed as a loose cultural grouping of various distinct and often opposed political units. Each of these clan and lineage groupings—often bitterly opposed to others by feud—has its own particular history. Yet certain broad trends are common and until recently the history of the Somali peninsula as a whole has been dominated by two themes: the southwards movement of the Somali at the expense of earlier populations, and the foundation and development by Arab and Persian settlers of a ring of coastal trading towns dating from at least the tenth century, and probably in some cases going back to Himyarite times.

In the sixteenth century these two separate lines of development merged to a considerable extent in the north. By this period the Muslim state of Adal, whose port was the Somali town of Zeila, had become the leader of a group of Muslim principalities in northern Ethiopia which were struggling for supremacy against the Christian Abyssinian kingdom. A turning-point in the previously inconclusive series of wars (dating from at least as early as the thirteenth century) was reached with the Abyssinian defeat in 1542 of the remarkable Muslim leader Aḥmad Grañ,[1] whose armies with their Somali contingents

[1] Aḥmad 'the left-handed', supposed by some, probably wrongly, to have been a Somali.

had harried Abyssinia almost to the point of collapse. This victory saved Abyssinia from Muslim conquest and led to the eventual decline of the Muslim states of North East Africa. It also closed the door to further Somali expansion to the west, and served to increase the already considerable pressure of the Somali thrust from north to south, which by this period had brought some Somali groups as far south as Merca on the Indian Ocean coast. With this stimulus too the Galla, many of whom had already given ground before the Somali tides of migration, swept wave after wave into Ethiopia, thus reducing the pressure of Galla resistance against the Somali and giving further encouragement to the southwards expansion of the latter.

It would be tedious and indeed pointless to trace here the continued Somali movement south over the next few centuries, which culminated in the settlement of Somali in Kenya as far south as the Tana River.[1] What is important, however, is that by the last decades of the nineteenth century prior to European intervention, the coastal and hinterland traditions had merged and the centre of political pressure had swung from the coast to the hinterland. In the north the ancient ports of Berbera and Zeila were now controlled by the nomadic Somali in whose territory they lay. On the southern Benadir coast, with the old ports of Merca, Mogadishu, and Brava, the position was very similar. Here the dominant political factor was now a tribe of the Rahanwiin family established with a hereditary dynasty on the lower reaches of the Shebelle River.

Political and commercial links which served to pave the way for European colonization had also, however, been forged between these coastal centres and the outside world. Zeila indeed was nominally part of the Turkish empire and was ruled by a Somali tributary of Oman. The towns of the southern coast, on the other hand, recognized the suzerainty of the Sultan of Zanzibar, although his effective local jurisdiction was nominal compared with that exercised on the spot by the Rahanwiin.

2. *The Imperial Partition*

In the years following the middle of the nineteenth century, the Somali peninsula was rapidly drawn into the theatre of

[1] For a fuller account see I. M. Lewis, 'The Somali Conquest of the Horn of Africa', *Journal of African History*, i. 2 (1960), pp. 213–29.

colonial competition between Britain, Italy, and France. On the African continent itself Egypt was also involved, and later Abyssinia, expanding and consolidating her realm at this period. Britain's direct interest in the Somali coast stemmed from her possession since 1839 of Aden as a coaling station on the short route to Imperial India. The Aden garrison found it impossible to obtain adequate local food supplies and was driven to import large shipments of meat from the Somali coast opposite. At the same time, there was a considerable Somali population in Aden, many of whom found employment with the British.

France, likewise, sought a Red Sea coaling station and managed to obtain Obock on the Danakil coast, later expanding eastwards and developing the Somali port of Jibuti. Italy, in her turn, opened a station at Assab on the coast of Eritrea in 1869, and this gradually increased in scope to become the Italian colony of Eritrea and a base for Italian infiltration into Ethiopia.

Faced with these European manœuvres in the era of aggrandizement under Ismail Pasha, Egypt revived Turkey's ancient claims to the Red Sea coast. And eventually, in 1869, the Egyptian flag was raised without significant local opposition at Bulhar and Berbera on the northern Somali coast. Britain at first protested at the Egyptian occupation of the Somali coast, but by 1877 had come to welcome the Egyptian settlement as a defence against the possible establishment of more hostile European powers opposite Aden. In 1884, however, the widespread disorganization produced by the Mahdi's revolt in the Sudan led Egypt (on British advice) to curtail her colonial responsibilities and abandon her Somali possessions. In these circumstances, and faced with French and Italian competition, to say nothing of the activities of the Germans and Russians, the British government reluctantly decided that Aden's security and the maintenance of her supplies necessitated a British occupation of the northern Somali coast.

Accordingly, although a number of Anglo-Somali commercial treaties already existed, the Aden authorities were instructed to prepare treaties of protection—which guaranteed the 'independence' of the signatories—with the principal northern Somali clans. These negotiations were successfully concluded in 1885 and 1886. The treaties themselves did not convey to Britain full rights over Somali territory, but a British protectorate was established, and a modest administration set up with officials who were styled Vice-Consuls and stationed in the ports of Zeila, Bulhar, and Berbera. The interior of the country was left undisturbed, and the Consul for the coast as a whole was stationed at Aden, the protectorate being initially under the authority of the India Office.

France meantime had been extending the scope of her small colony and a bitter wrangle soon developed with Britain over the delimitation of their respective territories. While at one time a solution by force seemed inevitable, this was averted and an Anglo-French agreement of 1888 decided where the boundary lay. This acknowledged that Zeila was within the British sphere. But the French loss was not great, for Jibuti became the capital of French Somaliland, and soon eclipsed Zeila with the construction of the line of rail linking the new port to the Ethiopian hinterland. Today the once prosperous city of Zeila is little more than a ruined town of crumbling mosques and tombs with only a small seasonally fluctuating population.

Stimulated by the continued Italian expansion of their Eritrean colony at his expense, the Abyssinian King Menelik in 1887 seized the Muslim city of Harar, which had been left independent after the Egyptian withdrawal in 1884, and incorporated it within his dominions. This brought Abyssinian pressure to bear directly upon the neighbouring Somali of whom many live in the vicinity of Harar. In 1889, under strong Italian pressure, the Abyssinians concluded with Italy the notorious treaty of Uccialli. This convention was generally accepted in Europe, though not wholeheartedly by France, as making Abyssinia into an Italian protectorate. In any event, with Italian capital and arms and ammunition, Menelik, who had succeeded to the title of Emperor of Abyssinia, proceeded to extend and consolidate his realm: to the east this process was largely at the expense of the Somali who, having no fire-arms, were in no position to resist effectively the attentions of well-equipped Abyssinian armies.

In the year in which the treaty of Uccialli was concluded Italy also established two Italian protectorates amongst the Majeerteen clan of the north-eastern part of the Somali peninsula.

And by the end of the year, the Imperial British East Africa Company, which had leased the Benadir coast from the Sultan of Zanzibar, sublet this region to an Italian Company. In 1892 this coast, with its ports of Mogadishu, Merca, and Brava, was directly let to the Italian company for an annual rent of 160,000 rupees. After the failure of this and a subsequent company administration in 1905, the Italian government assumed direct control of its colony of Somalia. To the south of the Juba River, the Imperial British East Africa Company retained its holding for the time being, but surrendered its charter after a Somali revolt in 1895 when Jubaland became part of the British East Africa Protectorate. Thus by 1889 the foreign partition of Somaliland was virtually complete, although many subsequent adjustments of territory amongst the new rulers took place.[1]

Now that the British and Italians were neighbours in Somaliland they had to define the extent of their respective holdings. In 1894 agreement was reached on the boundary between the two spheres but in 1897, following the resounding Abyssinian defeat of the Italians at the battle of Adowa in the previous year, the situation was radically changed. The Italian pretension to a protectorate over Ethiopia had collapsed and the European powers with interests in North East Africa clamoured to come to terms with Menelik. In 1897 France, Italy, and Britain all signed treaties with Ethiopia curtailing the extent of their Somali possessions to dimensions acceptable to the Emperor. For Britain and France other wider issues were at stake, the principal concern being the rivalry for control of the Nile, and the defeat of the Sudan Mahdists with whom Menelik's relations were ambiguous and threatening.

By her treaty Britain greatly reduced the size of her Somaliland Protectorate—there was even talk of giving it up altogether—and unilaterally abrogated her protectorate treaties with many sections of the clans whose independence she had undertaken to protect.[2] But the territory and people who were abandoned did not by the treaty become Ethiopian; no recognition by Britain of Ethiopian sovereignty was implied. Yet, of course, there was nothing now to stop their eventual subjection

[1] For more detailed discussion of the imperial partition of Somaliland, see *The Somali Peninsula: A New Light on Imperial Motives*, London, 1962.

[2] Most of the so-called Haud grazing area was given up. See below, p. 16.

by well-equipped Ethiopian armies. Italy, similarly, yielded the Ogaden region occupied by the Somali clan of that name to Ethiopia, although the boundary separating the Italian and Ethiopian spheres was not demarcated at the time. Agreement on this issue still remains a thorn in the flesh of both the Ethiopian and Somali governments today.

Thus 1897 saw the establishment of the French, British, and Italians in territorial areas acceptable to Ethiopia, if not equally approved by their Somali subjects, and the stage was set for the march of local events. For the next two decades these were dominated by the religious rebellion against the newly established Christian powers led by Sheikh Maḥammed ʿAbdille Ḥasan. This Somali sheikh of the Ogaadeen clan, born and brought up amongst his mother's people, the Ḍulbahante in the east of the British Protectorate, was an adherent of the Saaliḥiya Religious Order, one of the Muslim mystical brotherhoods,[1] and preached its reformist message with messianic zeal. He soon built up a considerable reputation for his learning, piety, and works, and gained fame as a mediator in clan and lineage disputes. In 1899, apparently for the first time, he came into contact with the work of Christian missionaries in the British Protectorate,[2] and about the same time he was involved in a petty dispute with the local administration over the alleged theft of a rifle. Contemporary Ethiopian and European encroachment and the example of the Mahdi of the Sudan caused these two incidents to grow into a major insurrection, with Sheikh Maḥammed as its leader.

The religious war which developed under the leadership of Sheikh Maḥammed, who assumed the title of 'Sayyid',[3] was in the main restricted to the northern part of the Somali peninsula. Only sporadic forays and risings by far-flung supporters of the Sayyid's cause occurred farther south. The French were not involved: most of the engagements were fought within the British Protectorate, although they overflowed into Italian and Ethiopian territory when these two powers lent their support to the British campaigns. However, as the poems in our collection

[1] On these movements in Somaliland, see below, pp. 29–30.

[2] The Foreign Office assumed administrative responsibility for the Protectorate in 1898. Prior to their assumption of control the India Office had forbidden entry to Christian missionaries.

[3] The title 'Mahdi' given him by some historians is not one which Somali apply.

reveal, the Sayyid's mission was directed against the Ethiopians and Italians as much as against the British.

Many of the British Protected Somali clansmen resisted the Sayyid's call to arms against the usurping 'infidels', especially those of the longer established Qaadiriya Muslim brotherhood which the Sayyid sought to supplant with his own Order, the Saaliḥiya. On the whole, despite his universalistic mission, most of his support was probably drawn from clansmen of the Daarood family to which his own clan belonged. But it is a mistake to imagine that he was denied Isaaq support, for often many of his followers belonged to this rival clan-family. And whatever their clan affiliation, all those Somali who aided the colonial governments, or who did not wholeheartedly throw in their lot with the Sayyid, were denounced as traitors to Islam.

With his own exceptional personal charisma and religious fame, however, Sayyid Maḥammed was remarkably successful in applying all the traditional devices of pastoral Somali politics, as well as the call to national Muslim solidarity, to build up a strong and flexible military organization which for twenty years defied the armies of his opponents. Thus while many Somali clans, according to the pressure of circumstances, now supported his followers and now turned against them, by employing daring guerilla tactics against the more cumbersome British armies the Sayyid's forces weathered four major British campaigns.[1] And when between 1910 and 1914 the British administration withdrew to the coast, abandoning the interior of the country to the Dervishes (as the Sayyid's followers were called), and to universal pillage, disorder, and famine, Sayyid Maḥammed seemed to have gained the day.

A new policy was subsequently adopted, however, and with a locally raised camel-constabulary the Dervishes were kept at bay until 1920, when a combined air, sea, and land assault routed them. The formidable stronghold at Taleh, built with the aid of Arab masons, was bombed, but Sayyid Maḥammed himself escaped with a few followers. Shortly after, however, while still desperately trying to rally his scattered supporters, the Sayyid died, probably of influenza or malaria and his movement finally collapsed.

[1] For a full account of these see D. Jardine, *The Mad Mullah of Somaliland*, London, 1923.

The Sayyid's rebellion had not achieved its aim of freeing his country from Christian interference, but it had successfully demonstrated the passionate attachment of Somali to Islam. It also served to impress forcibly upon the British Government the extraordinary resilience and pertinacity of the northern pastoral Somali. Its most lasting effect, however, was unfortunate, for it greatly strengthened the hand of conservative Somali opinion; and the Administration henceforth exercised the utmost caution, fearing that any progressive innovation might provoke a repetition of the Sayyid's rising.

After 1920 administrative control was gradually restored, the Colonial Office having in 1905 assumed responsibility for the Protectorate. In Italian Somaliland, where the effects of the holy war had been less strongly felt, the first fascist governor was appointed in 1923, and this marked a new positive phase in the administration and government of this costly and difficult colony, which hitherto had not fulfilled the optimistic aspirations of its first Italian colonizers. In 1925 the colony was extended by the cession of Jubaland from Britain, with the port of Kismayu, and this arrangement, which was part of the peace awards to Italy, unwittingly marked the first step in Somali unification. A year later the Italians concluded a military campaign against their two northern Somali protectorates and incorporated them firmly in the administrative structure of the colony.

For the next few years there is little of note to record, until 1935, when the Italian border dispute with Ethiopia at Walwal provided the Italians with the opportunity of launching their conquest of Ethiopia. Later events belong to recent history and need only be summarized. In 1940 the British Protectorate was evacuated, but recaptured with Italian Somaliland in 1941, and the two territories, with the Somali areas in Ethiopia, were then placed under British Military Administration. After the war the British Protectorate reverted to Colonial Office administration; the Haud and Ogaden regions were surrendered to Ethiopia,[1] whose jurisdiction over them Britain had come to recognize; and in 1950 the Italians returned to Somalia, which had been placed under United Nations Trusteeship, with ten years to prepare the country for independence. Social and

[1] The return of the Haud was a gradual process not completed until 1954.

political advancement was now rapid; and the effect was also felt in the British Protectorate, which, in the event, forestalled Somalia by becoming a sovereign state on 26 June 1960. On 1st July of the same year Somalia followed suit, and the two territories amalgamated to form the Somali Republic.

The great developments in all fields which these recent events imply have not, however, materially altered the basic issues of life. The life of the pastoral nomads who make up the majority of the population and which we describe in the following pages continues today in full vigour.

IV · PASTORALISM[1]

1. *Country and Water Resources*

The northern Somali pastoralists are engaged in a fierce and continuous struggle for survival. Much of the land over which they move with their livestock is semi-desert, inhospitable, and poorly endowed with the grazing and water resources which are essential for survival. Large tracts of country consist of barren plain, with a thin covering of vegetation only after rain. Elsewhere scrub bush abounds, including amongst its many varieties exotic gums and frankincense, and in places is almost impenetrably thick. Large trees are rare; but where they do occur in association with water they provide the sites for the often only semi-permanent trading settlements which are the oases of northern Somaliland.

Yet there are also lofty and magnificent ranges of mountains giving variety to the terrain which the northern pastoralists divide into three main topographical zones. There is first the barren coastal strip known as *Guban* (from *gub*, to burn). Here the average annual rainfall is about four inches, falling in the comparatively cool months between October and March and providing in good years a surprisingly generous covering of grass and vegetation. In the torrid months of summer the coast becomes unbearably hot and desiccated, and except in the main towns and ports is virtually deserted. Yet in all seasons water is relatively easily available just beneath the sandy topsoil. For the maritime hills which rise behind the coast are heavily

[1] For fuller information on the topics dealt with here, see I. M. Lewis, *A Pastoral Democracy*, London, 1961, pp. 31–90.

scarred by valleys carrying the northern run-off of the central highlands, the next zone distinguished by the pastoralists.

These highlands, with in places on the tops of the mountains vestigious forests of juniper, are known as *Ogo* (*Oogo*). This area, receiving much of its rain in the spring, is also fairly well-watered (on high ground the rainfall in places is twenty inches), but wells here have usually to be dug to a greater depth than on the coast. Wells which contain abundant water are used as the 'home-wells' for their grazing camels by those clans and lineages which in the winter dry season occupy this zone. From an altitude of over 6,000 ft. the highlands drop some 3,000 ft. as they slope southwards to the rich grazing lands of the Haud which form the third zone.

The Haud is a vast area of rolling plains and often red soil, interrupted in places by belts of thick scrub. It has no permanent water to match its excellent pastures, but many natural basins occur, and ponds have also been excavated, which become short-lived lakes after abundant rain. Here tall shady trees often grow and such sites are ideal for small seasonal trading posts. The water-pools themselves provide adequate water for human consumption and for the needs of the less hardy stock—sheep and goats, cattle, donkeys, horses, and burden-camels. But the water is too precious to use for the requirements of the herds of grazing camels, which are watered at the deep wells of the *Ogo* highlands. When the ponds themselves dry up, resort is had to the shallow wells which can usually be dug close to them. These too supply water for only a short time, and only in limited quantities, and are not opened to the grazing camels.

2. *The Seasons and Cycle of Movement*

As well as a host of local subsidiary seasons, there are four principal seasons, two wet and two dry. In the highlands and Haud generally the main rains are those of spring (*gu*), beginning about April in the west and usually coinciding with the onset of the South-West Monsoon. Ideally, this is the season of plenty when fresh green grass abounds and milk is plentiful. Stock-breeding is regulated so that most of the young are born at this time of year, and this is also the season of courting and of marriage, when there is a marked expansion in social life generally.

At the height of the South-West Monsoon winds, about June or July, with clouds of dust sweeping everywhere, the dry season of *ḥagaa* commences. The vegetation and pastures dry up more or less rapidly and the dry season pattern of watering begins. At the end of this trying season a short hot spell heralds the arrival of the autumn or *dayr* rains which fall in September or October and provide a subsidiary breeding season. The South-West Monsoon now drops and veers to the North-East. Generally, the rains are most abundant on the coast, where there may be scattered showers until December or January, when the harsh dry season of *jiilaal* begins in earnest. This is usually the severest period of the year, when livestock are likely to die of thirst or starvation and man's life is regularly threatened. Certainly the line between starvation and survival is narrow and precarious, and at best the pastoralists manage to keep alive at a bare subsistence level.

The annual cycle of movement conforms to the rotation of these four seasons and the pastoralists are keenly aware how rigidly their lives are governed by their hostile environment. In April or May, when the *Guban* becomes unbearably hot and dry, those who winter their flocks and herds on the coast retire up towards the highlands which have already been vacated by the clans whose home-wells and winter quarters are there. These central clans of the highlands have now moved into the Haud after the fresh new season's pasture. Although as the grass dries up there may be some return to the wells of the *Ogo* highlands, this distribution usually persists in broad outline until the autumn rains of September or October fall. Then the clans which winter on the coast move back there to enjoy the grazing which the rains have produced. And as this second rainy season rapidly gives place to the drought months of *jiilaal*, the pastoralists in the Haud retreat towards their home-wells and winter stations in the central highlands.

Although the availability of water and pasture and their distribution are the primary determinants of movement and grazing patterns, other factors are also significant. Amongst these are the prevalence of human or animal disease (seasonal malaria for example); the need to satisfy the salt requirements of the livestock; and such important human factors as the presence or absence of war and feud and administrative direction. As a whole the resultant pattern of movement is exceptionally fluid, and, except in relation to home-wells and trading settlements and towns, where the nomad trades his milk, skins, and stock for such essential supplies as sugar, tea, dates, rice, and clothes, there is little sense of attachment to territory. Pasture, in fact, is regarded as a gift from God to all Somali: and is not viewed as parcelled out amongst specified groups.

Kinsmen thus are normally not concentrated together on the same piece of land, but rather widely scattered with their livestock through the pastures. And it is mainly only when war and feud require the mustering of strength that kinsmen tend to congregate together. Indeed, ultimately the main factor governing the freedom of the individual in his pastoral movements is the necessity to be, if possible, within call of his kin should their help be required. Thus though the scarcity of water and pasture gives rise to innumerable disputes and feuds which sometimes smoulder on for generations, the overall pastoral picture is a fluid arrangement of men and their livestock on the land. Moreover, this pastoral system invades the small villages and trading centres which are widely distributed about the country. Even permanent townsmen, and there are few who spend all their days in the towns, have usually one foot in the interior where their livestock are with their kinsmen.

3. *The Herding Units*

In relation to their respective watering and pasture needs, the Somali pastoralists have developed a system of herding their stock in which the grazing camels are usually separated from the weaker stock—sheep and goats, cattle (if any), horses,[1] donkeys, and burden-camels. While feeding on dry grazing, sheep and goats must be watered every few days, while camels can do without water for twenty days or more. Consequently these two types of livestock are separated and herded in two distinct social units.

The nomadic hamlet (*guri* or *reer*)[2] consists of a group of families whose heads are close kinsmen, with their flocks, burden-camels to transport their tents (*aqal*) and effects, and

[1] The Somali pony, today much rarer than in the past decades, is still greatly prized for the prestige which its possession brings.

[2] The term *reer* also denotes a group of patrilineally related kinsmen.

occasionally a few milch camels or cattle. Material possessions are generally few and mainly utilitarian: the locally woven grass mats and skins and hides which, draped over semicircular wooden supports, form the nomad's collapsible hut or tent; wooden and fibre milking vessels and water-containers, plates and imported pots and pans; imported clothes and foodstuffs such as sugar, tea, dates, and rice or grain (mainly locally grown sorghum); and finally the nomad's weapons—knives, clubs, spears; and sometimes rifles and ammunition.

Thus constituted, the hamlet may be no more than the domestic group of a man, and wife (or wives), and their young children, with the livestock necessary for their support. Often, however, the hamlet consists of several such families, of brothers, or of other closely related men. In time of peace it is unusual to see a hamlet containing more than three or four families moving together, although in time of war larger groupings are often favoured for obvious reasons. Whatever its composition, the nomadic hamlet is led by the senior man of the predominant family within it.

Physically, the hamlet is a cluster of nomadic huts, or tents, grouped within a roughly circular fence of thornbush for protection against wild animals and other nocturnal enemies. Within the common enclosure are separate pens for the flocks of each of the component families. The care of the sheep and goats is essentially women's work, and from a tender age the girls of a hamlet are to be seen sheltering in the shade of a bush plaiting bark ropes and cords as they watch over the flocks at pasture, often a considerable distance from the camp.

While women attend to the needs of the flocks as well as being responsible for the loading and unloading of the burden-camels and the erection of the family tent, men assist them at the wells when the sheep and goats are watered. But the real focus of men's attention is the grazing camels for whose management they are solely responsible. Thus while girls stay at home helping with the flocks until they marry, boys from the age of seven years are sent out to the camel-camps to learn the stern art of camel husbandry. These camps consequently are in effect the initiation schools of the nomadic life. And here it should be remarked that, in contrast with many other African cultures, in Somaliland there is no formal system of initiation marking the transition from boyhood to manhood. However, Somali boys are circumcised, as elsewhere in Islam, either shortly after birth, or near puberty, to make them clean in a religious sense. But this is not an occasion for esoteric instruction, and is usually performed individually without much ceremony.

In the camel-camps which contain the pastoralists' favourite wealth, the camel-herders, boys and unmarried men—the sons, nephews, and younger brothers of the camel owners—live mainly on the milk of the beasts in their charge. Frequently they have no cooking facilities and sleep at night in the open, in a group, in the centre of the camp among the camels. Their life is generally frugal and arduous, and in the dry seasons when milk is scarce, often exceedingly hard. And in addition to the long treks which they have to undertake at regular intervals in the dry seasons to water the camels, and the frequent movement from pasture to pasture, they have to be constantly on the alert in case of raid or attack.

Physically the camel-camp is merely a large wide circle of high thorn fence divided into internal compartments in which the camels are lodged at night after the evening milking. It rarely contains more than four or five herds, each of about a hundred camels. And as with the hamlets, these are the stock of closely related kinsmen. Indeed the range of kinsmen who commonly have their camels together in the same camp is generally narrower than the range of those who move together in a nomadic hamlet. For more than sheep or goats, camels represent the corporate wealth of kinsmen, and unlike the former, which are individually branded, they usually bear the mark of a kinship group or clan section.

Wherever water and pasture are available, hamlets or camel-camps congregate in temporary settlements. These are not firm local units but merely ephemeral aggregations of people and stock. As the local pasture is exhausted and reports of better grazing and water elsewhere are received, they split up, individual hamlets or camel-camps, or parties of those of close kinsmen, moving off separately.

Because of the different needs and powers of endurance of their livestock, the nomadic hamlets and camel-camps usually have separate areas of movement. Thus a man may live with his wife and children and his flocks far from the pastures where his sons and younger brothers graze his camels. The grazing camels, indeed, may be seen only when they are brought in to water at wells near the area in which the hamlet is camped. But in the rainy seasons, and especially in the spring, the two herding units are likely to be close together, for when fresh green grass is abundant the flocks need no watering.[1] This, of course, is the most pleasant time of year when social life is at its height and the young camel-herders sally forth from their camps in the evening to go round the neighbouring hamlets serenading the girls with songs such as those on pp. 142–4. Dancing too is popular, and though not so common today as it seems to have been in the past, sometimes a young camel-herder fresh from the interior is so excited by the presence of the richly dressed young women that he becomes hysterically excited and, conventionally, is only quieted when the two sexes join in dance. Such dancing to relieve hysteria is accompanied by the singing of possession songs such as those on pp. 140–2. Incidents of this kind seem rare today when mixed dancing to songs like 'Dance Hunger' or 'The Best Dance' (pp. 142–4) is popular and more freely indulged in, apparently, than in the past. In the dry seasons, when hunger and preoccupation with the watering and pasture needs of the stock leave little room for frivolity, the two herding units usually draw apart and the camel-herders are again isolated from contact with the hamlets.

In addition to the constant movements from pasture to pasture and to the wells, every now and then caravans of camels have to be sent out to a trading post from the hamlets in search of supplies and to sell milk, and, in the dry seasons particularly, sheep- and goat-skins. For it is at this time of year when food is scarce that the pastoralists often kill sheep for food. The trading stations, some of which are almost as mobile as the people they serve, are connected with the main towns and coastal ports by motor transport, which has largely taken the place of the great camel caravans of the past. Many of the young men who leave the interior to seek work in the towns find employment as truck drivers. Their often dilapidated and ancient vehicles are to be seen plying up and down the dust tracks which serve as roads

[1] The use of motor vehicles to bring water to the flocks nowadays often allows the hamlets to remain longer in the southern pastures of the Haud, where the camels graze, than was formerly possible.

all over the country. A certain romance has grown up round this occupation, which is often arduous, and the modern song of today which is so popular on the radio (p. 144) seems to owe much in its development to ditties sung by truck drivers in the last few decades.[1]

V · SOCIAL ORGANIZATION

1. *Marriage and the Family*

Somali girls usually marry for the first time between the ages of fifteen and twenty; and men between eighteen and twenty-five. The choice of a bride is not a matter for the individual alone, and parents and elder kinsmen still exercise a considerable degree of control in match-making. Marriage is not merely an individual contract, it also unites the families and kinship groups of the couple.

The favourite season for seeking a bride is the spring, when the camel-camps and hamlets are close together, and the young camel-herders take advantage of this to serenade the girls of neighbouring hamlets, coaxing them to come and dance. Such occasions are generally highly restrained, for the pastoralists are puritanical in outlook and set a high value on virginity. Prior to marriage, a girl's virginity is safeguarded by infibulation which usually takes place about the age of ten, although sometimes it is performed earlier.[2]

Yet, however decorous, such fleeting contacts are often sufficient for a young man to select a girl whom he would like to marry. Girls are chosen for their physical beauty—particularly their posture, and the shape of their hips and bust; and a reddish-coloured skin and dark shining gums, are also considered to be especially attractive. But often of greater weight are such criteria as the standing and wealth of a girl's family and kinsmen, her own disposition and physical strength, and the advantages of the union in the wider context of clan politics.

The formal approach to the girl's family and request for her hand in marriage are made by an elder kinsman of the suitor. If the proposal is acceptable, the engagement of the couple is established by the presentation of a gift of livestock or money

[1] On the historical development of the modern Somali 'pop' song, see further below, p. 50.

[2] See I. M. Lewis, *A Pastoral Democracy* (1961), p. 44.

to the girl's family. Then the bridewealth proper is negotiated and paid, traditionally mainly in camels, of which a sum of thirty or more beasts constitutes a respectable payment. This gift evokes a corresponding return of wealth from the bride's family and kin to the kinsmen of the suitor. This dowry consists essentially of a few burden-camels laden with all the apparatus of the nomad's tent and furnishings to house the couple, and of a flock of sheep and goats to feed them and the children with which it is hoped their union will be blessed. It is also the responsibility of the bride's family to provide the wedding feast at their home, a celebration which often lasts seven days, and at which large numbers of guests have to be hospitably received.

The essential marriage contract, however, is not associated with the bridewealth, but consists of the undertaking which the husband makes before the sheikh or man of religion who solemnizes the marriage to give a small personal dower to his bride. This is often not paid at the time, and is frequently only honoured on divorce, if then. But this contract is the crux of the act of marriage. Thus when, as sometimes happens in a love-match of which the parents disapprove, the couple elope and are married privately, although the substantial bridewealth and dowry payments are dispensed with, the dower undertaking is not. Indeed, a detailed analysis of Somali marriage shows that while the dower agreement is the legal basis of marriage as an individual relationship between the couple, the bridewealth and dowry proper are concerned with the wider implications of marriage as an alliance between the families and kinship groups of the partners.[1]

The procedure outlined above is followed whether for a first or subsequent marriage. For as has been mentioned the Somali are polygynous and a man is enabled by Islam to have up to four wives at any one time. In practice the majority of men have only one wife, although there is a fairly high incidence of older men who have two, or more rarely, three or four wives.

Despite its elaborate character, marriage is not very stable and divorce is common, being more easily obtained by a man than by a woman. Of the many factors encouraging marital disharmony, one of the most serious is sterility attributed to a

[1] For a fuller discussion of this and other aspects of marriage, see I. M. Lewis *Marriage and the Family in Northern Somaliland*, London, 1962.

wife, for children, especially sons and heirs, are very highly prized. Thus here, as in so many other aspects, Somali women are at a disadvantage in relation to men, and this is but one aspect of their generally subordinate status. In inheritance women enjoy reduced rights, particularly in relation to livestock; and the standard rate of compensation payable when a woman is killed is fifty camels, half the corresponding amount for a man.

Yet, like their menfolk, Somali women are extremely independent, and find ways of making their influence felt. Moreover, in comparison with their sisters of the towns of other Muslim lands, in many respects their pastoral life allows them considerable freedom. Today, amongst townswomen, and especially the educated, there is a strong movement towards some improvement of their traditional position. These aspirations are generally favoured by the new educated classes of male society, and girls with schooling are much sought after and often command very high bridewealths, since women's education still lags far behind that of men.

2. *Extended Kinship Ties*[1]

The basic principle of social cohesion amongst the Somali is that based upon blood relationship traced through men in the male line. So that in the previous pages, when we have used the term 'kinsmen', we have meant people connected by common descent from a male ancestor. At each generation children receive an original first-name, and take as surname the first-name of their father. It is thus that the genealogies, which children learn from a tender age and in which the pastoralists take such pride, are built up.

Some initial conception of the way in which the whole fabric of Somali society is based upon descent and conceived in genealogical terms can be gained from the comparison which the pastoralists make of their use of genealogies with the European's use of addresses as different modes of identifying persons and groups. What a European's address is, they say, a man's genealogy is in Somaliland. And here we touch again on the fact that ties to locality are not strong or important amongst the pastoralists: it is not neighbours who support each

[1] For further information on the topics dealt with in this and the next section see, *A Pastoral Democracy*, especially Chs. 5–8.

other, if necessary with their blood, but kinsmen who are often widely scattered in different parts of the country.

Genealogies vary in their length with the strength of the group of kinsmen which they represent. The larger the groups are the longer their genealogy; the smaller they are the shorter their pedigree. The largest Somali groups which act corporately in a political sense we call 'clans', and these often have genealogies of twenty named generations or more, and a strength of as many as 100,000 individual members.

What is complicated about the pastoral Somali clan system is not its genealogical basis, but the fluid and shifting character of kinship groupings. Every ancestor with descendants in a man's pedigree represents, potentially at least, a point of unity and division. Thus clans are divided into many opposed groups of kinsmen who only unite in common cause when their clan as a whole is threatened. Indeed the bond of common patrilineal descent gives rise to almost limitless combinations and groupings of kinsmen; and it is the context of external hostility which, more than anything else, determines how people will act and in what corporate capacity.

Some degree of definition is given to this fluid picture by the fact that there is one unit, or level of kinship association, which more frequently than others is the basis of social and political interaction. This is the blood-compensation group (or 'dia-paying group'), a unit with a male population of a few hundred to a few thousand individuals who are all close kinsmen, and who recognize a common moral obligation to act as one man against outsiders. Most frequently this solidarity is stated—as it is evoked in practice—in relation to homicide. If a person is killed by a rival group, that group as a whole is liable to pay compensation to the offended group as a whole.

These and other obligations are detailed in formal treaties, today lodged in writing in the local offices of the Administration, which define the range of common responsibility binding the members of each group. Within each group, moreover, disputes are settled by the elders concerned and fines are levied on offenders. Thus within each group there is a rule of law. Outside and between groups, however, although all Somali recognize the same delicts, this is not so. But for the presence of an over-riding administration there would be no machinery with the power of enforcing its decisions to control the relations between groups. Hence, traditionally, while groups might have recourse to neutral arbitration, they were not compelled to do so, and if they wished they could disregard an arbitrator's judgement. Thus ultimately external relations depended upon the balance of power between groups, and the use of force, or its threat, in the end decided how disputes were settled.

Today the relative strengths of groups and the resort to force are still of the utmost importance in the pastoral political system. War and feud still often occur and have at their roots the fierce competition which prevails over access to the sparse grazing and water resources of the country. Moreover, Somali are traditionally warriors and have not lost their admiration for fighting prowess and strength of arms. These themes recur frequently in the serious poems included in this book.

It is hardly necessary to emphasize further how important superior political status, based on fighting potential, is under these conditions. What is interesting is the extent to which the Somali pastoralists are consciously aware of the importance of these factors in their lives, and how often their poems reflect philosophically, how, inevitably, military success breeds pride leading to disaster (see, e.g., pp. 104–10).

3. *Political Leadership*

In keeping with the fluidity of their social and political divisions, the pastoral Somali have no tradition of hierarchical government.[1] Their egalitarianism, indeed, is extreme, as anyone who has lived amongst them will know. At every level of association every adult man has the right to speak in the *ad hoc* councils which are formed to debate policy. Only women, and three categories of bondsmen (*sab*), all engaged in specialist crafts such as leather- and metal-working, and hairdressing, and forming only a small fraction of the population, were traditionally excluded from direct participation in these deliberations. Today, with universal adult suffrage and parliamentary government, attitudes are changing, and the position of these bondsmen is so changed that in many cases they enjoy the same rights as other men.

[1] Except in the coastal towns where the ruling dynasties of the past exercised some sporadic control of a very limited kind.

Moreover, although the larger blood-compensation groups have now government-paid headmen to act as a liaison between their kinsmen and the Administration, these officials have little real power. For there is no traditional office of group headman. And while in every group there are a few elders who command more respect than their peers, such men, however wealthy or distinguished in other respects, have no power to command others; only if they are lucky, can they persuade their colleagues.

Much the same must be said of the position of Sultan (*Garaad*, *Ugaas*, *Boqor*, &c.) or clan-head. This is traditionally a formal office, or perhaps rather, title, often vested in a particular lineage or clan section. Yet not every clan has such a Sultan, and amongst those who do, this leader is treated according to his personal power. Great leaders sometimes arise, but there is no continuity of formal political control, despite the idealized comparison which Somali often like to imply with Sultans in classical Arab literature.

Political groupings thus are fluid and fleeting; and government traditionally is exceptionally democratic in this warring society, where the security of the individual is determined ultimately by the number and strength of kinsmen whom he can summon to his support.

VI · RELIGION: THE SOMALI PRACTICE OF ISLAM

1. *Theology*

The northern pastoralists display a deep attachment to Islam and a strength of devotion which recalls the fervour and puritanism of early Islam. As Sunnis they adhere to the orthodox tradition of the Prophet and his 'Community', while in doctrine and law they follow the Muslim jurist ash-Shaafi'ii. Thus Islam is a vital force and the regular religious duties are taken seriously: the daily prayers (most scrupulously observed by the old), alms-giving to the poor, the feast of Ramadan, pilgrimage to Mecca, and the confession of the faith: 'There is no God but Allah, and Muḥammad is His Prophet'. These words spring readily to their lips at all times and the omnipotence of God is constantly recognized.

Certainly, notwithstanding their highly developed sense of

independence, the pastoralists hold steadfast in the belief that God is the ultimate source of causation, and conceive of their Creator as a largely impersonal power in whose sight man is helpless and impotent. To Somali, God is remote, all-powerful, judging and just, and men turn to Him in sorrow and distress, as well as in joy and thanksgiving. Sickness and health, good and ill fortune, all exist with his consent and are in his power to withhold or bestow. And although magico-religious procedures based chiefly upon the mystical power of the Quran are applied in the treatment of disease, illness and misfortune are rarely ascribed to magical causes. Yet neither are they necessarily regarded as a direct reflection of Divine wrath. For awards and punishments do not automatically fall due in this life, but may be received after death on the day of judgement. Man in any case is held to be by nature sinful and wayward, so that God's displeasure is assumed as a constant condition, rather than viewed as an immediate punishment for a particular transgression. Thus worldly success is not necessarily taken as a sign of God's favour. Indeed the pastoralists incline to a puritanical and ascetic view of the transitory character of mundane achievement, a theme often expressed in poetry (see, e.g., p. 110).

Despite their orthodoxy there tends to be, as elsewhere, some latitude between religious principle and conventional practice. Thus Somali do not follow to the letter all the regulations of the Shafiʿite code of Muslim law. Where there is serious conflict between Islamic rulings and the demands of customary practice, the latter often prevail. In the inheritance of property, for example, the pastoralists usually lay greater emphasis upon the legal rights of men and of patrilineal kinsmen at the expense of women and maternal relatives than is fully consonant with the provisions of the Shafiʿite code. This is especially the case in the inheritance of camels. Again, although the Shafiʿite code stipulates that a person who is guilty of deliberate homicide is alone responsible for making reparation, the pastoral practice is for joint responsibility to be accepted by the culprit's blood-compensation group. Nor is this a matter of popular ignorance, for the nomads are here well aware that their practice is contrary to the religious law.

Thus there tends to be a certain degree of conflict between

the ideal tenets and ordinances of Islam and customary practice. But this in no way diminishes the firm attachment of the Somali pastoralists to their faith. Indeed, so basic is this in their life and culture, that to some extent Islam has become a vehicle for the expression of their formidable sense of pride and individuality as a people. Thus Islam reinforces the cultural nationalism of the Somali.

2. *The Veneration of Saints*

Although the pastoralists regularly honour God through the Prophet in prayer, praise, and sacrifice, they feel generally far removed from Him and rely heavily upon Muslim saints to intercede with Him on their behalf. The cult of saints (Sufism—the mystical movement in Islam) is strongly developed, in its external rather than esoteric aspects. This to a large extent is consistent with the clan and lineage organization of pastoral society.[1] For the ancestors of large and important clans are venerated as Muslim saints, whatever they may in fact have been in their own times, and are thus in effect canonized in Islam.

Not all the saints venerated in regularly performed services, sacrifices, and pilgrimage to their tombs, however, are lineage ancestors. Of religious authority equal to that of such ancestors as Sheikhs Daarood and Isaaq,[2] founders of the corresponding clans, are the founders of the Religious Orders which the Somali follow. The main locally important Orders are the Qaadiriya and Aḥmadiya, both widespread in the Islamic world generally, and highly orthodox. The first, indeed, is the oldest Religious Order in Islam, with its historical centre at Baghdad, while the second is a reformist movement founded in Arabia in the late eighteenth century.

All Somali belong to one or other of these Orders, or to their subsidiary branches, such as the Saaliḥiya division of the Aḥmadiya followed by Sheikh Maḥammed ʿAbdille Ḥasan. And although only a few Somali are full initiates, adherence to these Orders is practically synonymous with the profession of the faith. The Orders themselves have a somewhat informal

[1] For further information see I. M. Lewis, 'Sufism in Somaliland: A Study in Tribal Islam', *Bulletin of the School of Oriental and African Studies*, 1955 and 1956.

[2] A popular northern Somali praise-hymn for Sheikh Isaaq is included on pp. 153–8.

hierarchical organization of clergy and have a national membership cutting across sectional divisions in the clan system. Thus the members of different and often hostile lineages or clans frequently follow the same Order. But the loyalties so created are weak compared with the compelling bonds of kinship identity; and where there is a conflict of loyalties it is the latter which usually prevail.

The existence of these Orders, and the extensive development of saint veneration through them and through the ancestors of clans as well as through other men who acquire the status of saints for their personal works and piety, in no sense weakens the power of God or detracts from the pre-eminence of the Prophet. For it is a measure of the lofty absoluteness of God that, in their appeals to Him through the Prophet, men seek the intercession of those who have found favour in His sight. Thus the doctrine of the Aḥmadiya holds that 'Sayyid Aḥmad (their founder) is in the door of the Prophet, and the Prophet in the doorway of God'.

3. *The Role of Men of Religion or Sheikhs*

Although the pastoral Somali have so strong a warrior tradition, not all men are warriors. Indeed Somali draw a general distinction between men of religion or sheikhs[1] on the one hand, and warriors (*waranle*, literally 'spear-bearer') on the other. While the majority of men are 'warriors', a minority who, however else they may gain a livelihood, practise as religious experts, fall into the category of men of religion. By definition, if not always in practice, such persons are excluded from full participation in secular affairs, especially from secular politics and fighting; and ideally the role assigned to them is that of mediation between man and man, and man and God. Thus whether they hold religious office in one of the Orders or not, men of God are concerned with the conduct of the religious life of the group in which they live.

They solemnize marriage, officiate at funerals, lead the weekly Friday prayers, and direct all religious activities and ceremonies. Many of them give religious instruction, teaching Arabic and

[1] In Somali *wadaad*. This term and the Arabic loan-word 'sheikh' are used interchangeably, although the latter title tends to be given to the better educated and more learned of *wadaads*.

the elements of Muslim theology and law. They are also much in demand for prophylactic charms and potions, and in clan politics act as mediators and peace-emissaries. For all these tasks they are rewarded by gifts, and some men of religion live almost entirely on charity. This is in full accordance with Somali ideas of the blessing which attaches to asceticism, and generally those men of religion who renounce worldly pursuits and ambitions are considered as the most pious and most favoured in the sight of God. These devout attitudes towards those who devote their lives to God's work, it must be added, do not prevent warrior pastoralists from regarding men of religion on other occasions as tiresome parasites.

In keeping with their ideal (if only partly fulfilled) role of neutrality and divorcement from worldly affairs, men of religion are considered to enjoy a certain measure of mystical protection against wanton attack. It is not only dishonourable but also even dangerous to molest the person or property of a 'poor' man of God. And here we touch upon a wider Somali notion that those who are weak in worldly power and mundanely helpless have, in compensation, a special endowment of mystical power. The meek enjoy the blessing of God.

Thus men of religion are in a sense complementary to warriors and stand for the transcendental values of Islam which unite Somali over and above the sectional clan interests which divide them. Consequently, in contrast to the position in some other tribal Muslim communities, sheikhs are not leaders in secular politics. But when an issue is of national importance and threatens the Muslim basis of Somali culture, they can assume temporary positions of politico-religious authority. The best recent example of this is the case of Sayyid Maḥammed ʿAbdille Ḥasan who so effectively defied the Ethiopian, British, and Italian 'infidel' authorities in the holy war which he led against them between 1900 and 1920.[1]

Yet when such opportunities for the mobilization of widespread religious indignation are absent, men of religion cannot command such influence. Indeed, despite their ideal divorcement from worldly attachments and their frequent denunciation of feud and war within the Muslim Somali community, inevitably they find themselves drawn into the disputes which concern

[1] See above, pp. 12–14.

their warrior kinsmen. For although a few men of God live in geographically self-contained religious communities, the majority live as nomads cheek by jowl with their warrior kinsmen, upon whom ultimately they depend for their security: for their mystical protection in itself is not a sufficient guarantee of safety. And, as with warriors, they are members of the warrior blood-compensation groups which define and circumscribe the political and social status of every individual in this insecure pastoral life. Only a handful of sheikhs of exceptional piety deny their kinship affiliations and have thereby contracted out of society.

VII · CONCLUSIONS

This brief outline may, we hope, serve to give the reader some idea of at least the more important and characteristic features of the social and cultural setting of Somali poetry. And certainly some reference to most of the themes touched upon here will be found in the poems which follow. With the style and structure of the poems themselves, and the main features of the Somali language, we deal in a following section, in which we also include brief biographical sketches of our main authors.

But before leaving this introduction to the life of the pastoral nomads it will be as well to re-emphasize that this nomadic existence continues today with undiminished vitality. The great social and political changes of the last few decades have not altered the essential features of northern Somali pastoralism. And to some, no doubt, it will seem strangely incongruous that in the tea-shops of trading posts in the far interior pastoralists from the Haud eagerly listen to the competing radio voices of Cairo, Moscow, and London, as well as to local Somali broadcasting stations, and compare the relative merits of popular songs, such as those on p. 144, with the older forms of verse from which these have developed. Yet this is the case and in many ways typifies the ebb and flow of contact and innovation between town and interior, and between the new and the old, which is characteristic of life in the Somali peninsula today.

B · THE SOMALI LANGUAGE

1 · PLACE OF SOMALI AMONG THE LANGUAGES OF AFRICA

Of the systems of classification which have been proposed[1] relating Somali to the other languages of Africa, that adopted in the *Handbook of African Languages*[2] appears at the moment to be most satisfactory. This places Somali in the Cushitic group which comprises some thirty languages and dialect clusters spoken in North-Eastern Sudan, Eritrea, French Somaliland, Ethiopia, the Somali Republic, and the Northern Frontier District of Kenya. Of this group the most widely spoken are Somali and Galla. Indeed the speakers of these two languages together greatly outnumber the speakers of all the remaining Cushitic languages and dialect clusters. Within the Cushitic group Somali is closely allied to Galla (spoken in Ethiopia and in the Northern Frontier District of Kenya) in grammatical structure, and to a lesser extent in vocabulary, where there is about twenty per cent resemblance.

The relationship between Somali and the other Cushitic languages (with the exception of Rendille)[3] is more distant. It amounts to the sharing of certain grammatical features and a measure of common vocabulary. Thus, for example, the Cushitic Danakil-(ʿAfar-)speaking tribes are geographically as close Somali neighbours as the Galla, and in many respects culturally very similar, yet the relationship between Somali and Danakil is more remote than between Somali and Galla.

In the present state of our knowledge it seems most satisfactory to regard the Cushitic language group as a part of a family of languages, including Berber, Ancient Egyptian, and Semitic.[4] This placement of the Cushitic group is based upon

1 For discussion of this subject see 'Problèmes de typologie dans la classification des langues non-bantu de l'Afrique du Nord-Est', by A. N. Tucker, *Journal de la Société des Africanistes*, 1961, pp. 59–74.

2 The relevant volume is Part III of the Handbook, *The non-Bantu Languages of North-East Africa*, by A. N. Tucker and M. A. Bryan, 1956, published by the International African Institute.

3 The Rendille are a people of part Somali origin, some 25,000 strong, in the Northern Frontier District of Kenya. Their language is even closer to Somali than Galla.

4 As postulated by A. N. Tucker and M. A. Bryan in their *Linguistic Analyses*—

similarity of grammatical characteristics, and, to a very small extent, of vocabulary. The evidence points to a possible common origin for the family as a whole, but this has not yet been definitely established, in spite of a great deal of research. It is difficult to go beyond this at the moment. No one has yet succeeded in satisfactorily demonstrating a system of regular sound correspondences on which a theory of common origin could be legitimately based. It is, of course, possible that future work may reveal a relationship of a very different kind from that familiar in Indo-European studies.

II · MAIN CHARACTERISTICS OF THE SOMALI LANGUAGE

The Somali language is remarkably rich in grammatical structures and vocabulary. Nominal and verbal formations have numerous affixes with a variety of grammatical functions, providing a wide range of subtle distinctions and shades of meaning. Unlike those of Bantu languages, the inflexions normally follow roots instead of preceding them. Only five verbs in the entire language diverge from this norm: these exceptions, like Semitic verbs, have both prefixes and suffixes.

The language has two genders; and in nouns the plural forms usually reverse the gender of the singular. Thus *gabaḍ* 'girl' is feminine in the singular, but the plural *gabḍo* 'girls' is masculine. Gender in nouns is bound up with verbal concord. This is extremely complex, since rules apply in main sentences different from those in the dependent clauses. Moreover, the type of concord varies according to the presence or absence of certain particles in the sentence.

Nouns and nominal formations (such as nouns followed by dependent clauses, taken as units) have a case system of a very unusual type, in which the case signs vary according to their syntactic positions.[1]

The verbal forms are characterized not only by a well differentiated inflectional system indicating person, number,

Non-Bantu Languages of North-Eastern Africa, *Handbook of African Languages*, Part IV (in the press).

[1] This is briefly discussed in the introduction to *Ḥikmad Soomaali* by M. Ḥ. I. Galaal, edited, with grammatical introduction and notes, by B. W. Andrzejewski, Annotated African Texts IV, School of Oriental and African Studies, O.U.P. 1956. A detailed description can be found in *Declensions of Somali Nouns* by B. W. Andrzejewski, School of Oriental and African Studies, London, 1964, distribution by Luzac & Co., London, W.C. 1. (in the press).

and tenses, but also by derivational classes comparable to the 'Derived Verbs' of Arabic. The same root occurs usually in two or more classes and in the majority of cases a specific category of meaning is shared by the class. Thus, for example, the majority of verbs ending in *-i* in the imperative singular are causatives, while those ending in *-o* are associated with the meaning of 'doing something for oneself'.

Another important feature, shared with Galla and Rendille, is that the accentual features, consisting of stress and intonation, are correlated with grammatical categories. Thus verbal paradigms and noun forms of various types have their own specific accentual patterns: all the forms of the present tense general, for example, have a different accentual pattern from that of the forms of the present tense continuous. Similarly, the gender of nouns, in certain syntactic positions, is distinguished by accentual pattern, e.g. *ínan* 'boy' and *inán* 'girl'. Singular and plural forms are also sometimes differentiated in the same way, e.g. *díbi* 'ox', *dibí* 'oxen'. Moreover, the accentual pattern is frequently bound up with the system of nominal concord and serves to distinguish subject from non-subject, e.g. *nín bàa más diláy* 'a man killed a snake' and *nín bàa mas dilay* 'a snake killed a man'.

Since the accentual patterns are a part of grammatical structure they cannot also be used, to the same extent as in English and some other languages, to convey various 'shades of meaning' and emphasis. Instead, this is achieved in Somali by the use of various particles which play a pivotal role in the language.

III · VOCABULARY

The wealth of the vocabulary depends not only upon the existence of a large number of distinct roots but also upon the very high productivity of the derivational system. Thus one root often yields a whole cluster of verbs of different conjugations and also supplies a group of nouns of different type. Two layers are apparent in the vocabulary: one contains words of everyday speech, while the other is a repository of words no longer in current use, but of frequent occurrence in poetry. This poetic vocabulary, though widely known by the nomads of the interior, is often unintelligible to many of the younger generation of townsmen. And the latter, lacking the knowledge as part of their upbringing, have in many cases had to learn this special vocabulary in later life in order to understand and appreciate the traditional poetic forms. Moreover, today it is particularly this poetic vocabulary which is being drawn upon to provide words and expressions to meet the new demands of modern social and political change. Archaic words are increasingly being restored to current use, often with slightly modified meanings. Thus the obsolescent word *ḥoghaye* has acquired the meaning 'secretary' and the word *marwo*, an old praise word for a married woman, is being sometimes applied in its modern sense, more or less equivalent to the English 'lady'.

In a wider sense still the Somali language as a whole is showing remarkable adaptability.[1] Old roots from both the general and more specialized vocabulary layers have been utilized to create entirely new words, many of which have become a part of the language. The following are typical examples: *dayaḥga'meed* 'artificial satellite' (lit. '*hand-made moon*'), *hantiwadaag* 'socialism' (lit. 'wealth-sharing'), *warsidde* 'newspaper' (lit. 'news carrier'), *horumar* 'progress' (lit. 'moving forward'), *hubka halista ah* 'nuclear weapons' (lit. 'weapons which are of extreme danger').

In this sphere of innovation the radio has played a very significant part. Somali broadcasters take special pride in preserving the purity of their language and in expressing new concepts and ideas avoid foreign borrowings as far as possible. All this indicates something of the resourcefulness and richness of the Somali language. However, in keeping with the longstanding attachment of the Somali to Islam, and centuries of contact with Arabia, Arabic has exerted a marked influence on the Somali language. Its impact has been greatest in vocabulary. A large number of words, especially those connected with Islam and urban civilization, are Arabic borrowings. Typical examples from a very large number of such words are: *soon* 'fasting', *kitaab* 'book', *markab* 'ship', *suldaan* 'sultan'. This Arabic influence still continues and in

[1] For an interesting demonstration of this see M. M. Maino, *La lingua somala-strumento d'insegnamento professionale*, Alessandria (Italy), 1953; and M. M. Maino and Yasin 'Isman Kenadid, *Terminologia medica e sue voci nella lingua somala*, Alessandria, 1953.

addition to pure Somali roots, modern Arabic words relating to recent social and political developments have also gained currency. Examples are words like *jariidad* 'newspaper', *sawd* 'vote', and *shuu'i* 'communist'.

Despite the association between Islam and Arabic, there has always been some resistance to accepting Arabic importations as opposed to pure Somali roots. This conflict between traditional Somali cultural nationalism on the one hand and attachment to Islam on the other has given rise to many problems, not least those connected with the choice of a script for writing Somali.[1] Not surprisingly, even greater resistance has been shown to the adoption of foreign loan-words from English, French, Italian and Amharic, languages of the colonial powers. Nevertheless, in each of the areas either in the past or still today associated with a particular foreign administration certain borrowings have gained a limited currency.

The extent to which the Somali language has borrowed words from the adjacent Galla and Danakil-speaking peoples is still obscure. The issue raises the wider problem of the precise historical connexion between these three languages and their general position within the Cushitic group. At present there is often no means of determining whether a particular word common to these languages is a borrowing or whether it derives from a common stock.

IV · DIALECT DIVISIONS

The Somali language comprises a number of dialects which can conveniently be grouped in three main divisions:

1. Common Somali.
2. Central Somali.
3. Coastal (Benadir) Somali.

By Common Somali we mean the dialect type understood throughout the Somali Peninsula and spoken by the majority of the pastoral nomads who make up the bulk of the Somali nation. This is the dialect type found everywhere except in the cultivation area between the Juba and Shebelle rivers, occupied

[1] See E. Cerulli, 'Tentativo indigeno di formare un alfabeto somalo', *Oriente Moderno*, vol. xii, Genn.-Dic., 1932; and I. M. Lewis, 'The Gadabuursi Somali Script', *Bulletin of the School of Oriental and African Studies*, vol. xxi/i.

by the Digil and Rahanwiin tribes (speaking Central Somali), and except in the Southern coastal towns (Merka, Brava, Warsheikh and Mogadishu) and their environs, where Coastal Somali is spoken. Even in the areas where Central and Coastal Somali are spoken Common Somali has generally the status of a lingua franca.

As has already been explained it is particularly in the dialects of Common Somali that poetry is most strongly developed and it is from this dialect type that our collection is chosen.

Central Somali, the dialect type of the predominantly cultivating Digil and Rahanwiin tribes, differs from Common Somali to something like the extent Italian differs from Spanish or Russian from Polish: they become mutually intelligible if their speakers are in close contact for a few months.

Coastal Somali has a simpler grammatical structure than the other two dialect groups and it is much nearer to Common Somali than to Central Somali; the speakers of Common Somali and Coastal Somali can normally understand each other, with only occasional difficulties in communication. The area of currency of Coastal Somali is a little less extensive than that of Central Somali.[1]

V · TRANSCRIPTION

The Somali language has no official and generally accepted orthography. Although several systems of writing it are in existence, none has established itself firmly.

Adaptations of the Roman and Arabic alphabets have been launched and entirely new scripts have been invented, but each of them has met with very strong, sometimes violent, opposition on the part of those who either favoured a rival system or did not want to see Somali written at all.

It is most unfortunate that the problem of writing Somali has always been bound up with conflicting trends in Somali society and that any particular views in this matter are regarded as indicative of a personal political and religious outlook. Some people even go so far as to reject the idea of written Somali and would prefer to establish Arabic as the national language

[1] For a discussion of Somali dialect division see M. M. Moreno, *Il somalo della Somalia, grammatica e testi del Benadir, Darod e Dighil*, Rome, 1955.

and to reduce Somali to the role of a 'vernacular' second language. But since the creation of the Somali Republic, by the unification of the former British Somaliland Protectorate and ex-Italian Somalia, the need for a Somali orthography has become pressing, as officials with British education usually do not have a written language in common with those of Italian education. They all speak Somali, but often have to employ translators in order to read correspondence between government offices. Aware of the urgency of the matter the Somali Government set up in 1961 a Linguistic Committee to investigate the problem and the public were invited to submit their proposals. Some eighteen systems were submitted, and after long deliberation and study the committee presented its recommendations to the Government. At the moment of writing the matter still awaits the Government's decision and it is possible that it will first be brought before the National Assembly for discussion and approval. No one can foresee, however, how the problem will eventually be solved. At the moment the main rivals in the contest are the supporters of an orthography based on the Roman alphabet and those who would like to introduce a Somali script called Osmania (*ʿUsmaaniya*) and also known as Somali Writing (*Far Soomaali*), invented some forty years ago. The latter have been very active particularly since the Second World War, and even make use of a specially designed typewriter keyboard.

Having no official orthography at our disposal, we have to make our own decision on the transcription of Somali. On the grounds of convenience and economy, we have adopted a system evolved by Mr. Shirreh Ahmed Jama (Shire Aḥmed Jaamaʿ) of Mogadishu, which does not require any special letters and which can easily be read by anyone familiar with the Somali language. All the texts of the poems and all the extracts from poems in the introduction are transcribed in this system. The only difficulty that occurs because of our choice of this system is that certain letter symbols such as *c* and *ch* are used to represent Somali sounds and not their English or Italian equivalents, and this might confuse a reader unacquainted with Somali. Therefore, when Somali words, including proper names occur in the English translation and in the introduction (except for quotations of whole passages of poetry) they are written according to the spelling system adopted in *A Pastoral Democracy* by I. M. Lewis. The system differs very little from that of Shirreh Jama, as will be shown below.

The two systems of transcription used in this book can best be described by reference to some of the existing systems on which published information is available.[1] In common with the systems evolved by ʿAbdullāhi Hhāji Mahhamūd and Bruno Panza, B. W. Andrzejewski,[2] C. R. V. Bell, M. M. Moreno and in common with that of Somali Writing, Shirreh Jama and I. M. Lewis show only five basic vowel qualities: *i*, *e*, *a*, *o*, *u*. Like Lilias E. Armstrong, B. W. Andrzejewski, and C. R. V. Bell, they differentiate the length of vowels by using single letters for short vowels and double letters for long vowels. Thus the short *i*, *e*, *a*, *o*, *u* correspond to long *ii*, *ee*, *aa*, *oo*, *uu*. The double vowel letters in the transcriptions of Shirreh Jama and I. M. Lewis correspond therefore to vowel letters marked with a macron (*ī*, *ē*, *ā*, *ō*, *ū*) in the transcription of ʿAbdullāhi Mahhamūd and Bruno Panza, and to the letters marked either with a macron or with a circumflex in the transcription of M. M. Moreno.

The consonant symbols are the same as in the systems of ʿAbdullāhi Mahhamūd and Bruno Panza, Lilias E. Armstrong, C. R. V. Bell, M. H. I. Galaal and B. W. Andrzejewski, and M. M. Moreno, except for the differences set out in the table below:

ʿAbdullāhi Mahhamūd and Bruno Panza . . .	dh	sh	j	kh	hh	ʻ		y
Lilias E. Armstrong . .	ɖ	ʃ	j	x	ħ	ʿ	ʾ	**y**
C. R. V. Bell . . .	ɖ	sh	j	kh	ħ	ʿ	ʾ	y
M. H. I. Galaal and B. W. Andrzejewski . . .	ɖ	sh	j	kh	ħ	ʿ	ʾ	y, y̌
I. M. Lewis . . .	ḍ	sh	j	kh	ḥ	ʻ	ʼ	y
M. M. Moreno . . .	ḍ	š	ǧ	ḫ	ḥ	ʿ	ʾ	y
Shirreh Jama . . .	dh	sh	j	kh	ch	c	ʼ	y

It should be noted that in the system of ʿAbdullāhi Mahhamūd and Bruno Panza, and in Somali Writing there is no

[1] Bibliographical references will be given on pp. 59–60.

[2] As in the 'Broad Transcription' suggested for orthographic purposes in 'The problem of vowel representation in the Isaaq dialect of Somali'; see p. 59.

symbol for the glottal stop (hamza), represented by others as ʾ or ’. The distinction between *y* and *ÿ*, which is discussed in the introduction to *Ḥikmad Soomaali*, is disregarded in all the other systems.

Readers who are not familiar with any of the works quoted above, but know either Somali writing or the Arabic alphabet as used for Somali, may find it helpful to consult this conversion table:

Somali Writing . . .	[illegible]	[illegible]	[illegible]	[illegible]	[illegible]	[illegible]		[illegible]
Arabic alphabet . . .	ڎ	ش	ج	خ	ح	ع	ء	ي
Shirreh Jama . . .	dh	sh	j	kh	ch	c	.	ÿ
I. M. Lewis . . .	ḍ	sh	j	kh	ḥ	‘	’	y

Although Shirreh Jama's system provides symbols for representing the sounds of Somali, it is not yet known what spelling conventions and word-division rules are to be attached to it. In view of this we have followed the method which is explained in detail in the introduction to *Ḥikmad Soomaali*. One of the most important features of this system is that the final vowels of words have variants according to their positions in relation to sounds which follow immediately. Thus in *ma haysto* 'I don't have', *haysto* ends in *o*, but in *ma haysto e*, 'but I don't have', it ends in *e* (*ma hayste e*), assimilating to the conjunction *e*. Similarly *maro* 'cloth', but *maro ḍeer* (*mara ḍeer*) 'long cloth', where in the first case the final vowel of *maro* is followed immediately by a pause and in the second by a consonant. According to the method used in *Ḥikmad Soomaali* the alternating vowels are uniformly spelt with a letter which represents the quality which they have when immediately followed by a pause, leaving it to the reader to make the appropriate adjustments.

C · CHARACTERISTICS OF SOMALI VERSE AND BIOGRAPHICAL NOTES ON POETS

I · ALLITERATION

THE most striking feature of Somali poetry, which can be noticed even by a person who does not know the language, is its alliteration, called in Somali *higgaad*. In every hemistich of a poem[1] at least one word has to begin with a chosen consonant or with a vowel.

The rules of alliteration are very rigid in the sense that only identical initial consonants are regarded as alliterative (*higaad-san*) with one another and no substitution by similar sounds is admissible. All initial vowels count as alliterative with each other, and again this principle is most strictly observed.

The same alliteration is maintained throughout the whole poem. If, for example, the alliterative sound of a poem is the consonant *g*, in every hemistich there is one word beginning with *g*. A poem of one hundred lines (two hundred hemistichs) will therefore contain two hundred words beginning with *g*.[2] Similarly, if the alliterative sound is a vowel, in every hemistich there is one word beginning with a vowel.

The two passages below illustrate these principles; the first alliterates in *g* and the second in a vowel.

Dhaachaan ka gabangaabsaday e   waygu geliseen e
Gooddiga Ban Cawl buu fakhrigu   geed ku leeyahay e
Gaajada huggeedii miyaa   galabta i saaray?

I lately sought this plight for myself and you put me into it,
On the edge of the ʿAwl Plain, poverty has a tree (to sit under),
Have the garments of hunger been put on me this evening?[2]

Afkaagan wanaagsan
Udgoonkiisiyo araggaan
Ubachaay, u oolaa.

[1] If the poem consists of short lines undivided by a caesura every line may contain only one alliterative word.

[2] This extract from a poem by ʿAli Ḥammaal inspired Margaret Laurence to choose the title 'A Tree for Poverty' for her anthology of Somali verse (see Select Bibliography, p. 60).

1 (It is because of) your fine mouth,
2 Its scent and sight,
3 That I postpone my journey,[1] oh Flower!

The rules of alliteration also include certain restrictions on the type of words which can be used: they must be words with readily assignable meanings, such as nouns, numerals, proper names, or verbs. Prepositional particles, conjunctions, or emphasis and concord particles such as *baa* or *waa* are not regarded as suitable for alliteration and any one using them is considered as falling short of the standards required of a poet.

II · POETIC DICTION

It is not unreasonable to conjecture that the exacting demands of alliteration, maintained throughout the whole poem, have had a profound influence on Somali poetic diction. The poet, to supplement his store of words, has to resurrect archaic words, enliven obsolescent ones, and even create new ones, and many arguments arise among Somali audiences as to the precise meanings of such archaicisms as are used in poetry. There is obviously even greater opportunity for differing interpretations in the case of newly coined words, where sometimes even the poet himself can be evasive when asked to explain them.

Alliteration often leads a poet through a chain of purely acoustic associations into unexpected regions of thought and imagery, and unless he is a master of his craft it will carry him far away from his main theme. As a young western-educated Somali once said, a weak poet, trying to alliterate in 'm', will drag his audience on a tortuous and pointless journey from Mogadishu to Milan, via Mombasa, Manchester, Madagascar, Monrovia, and Moscow.

While such poets find the restrictions of alliteration an insurmountable obstacle, men with real talent dazzle their audiences with their powers of expression, undiminished by the rigidity of the form. Yet even in their poetry the poetic images are not connected by any very obvious logical sequence, and the meaning of whole lines can often only be guessed from the general trend of the poem.

For the Somalis, listening to poetry is thus not only an artistic pleasure, but provides them with the fascinating intellectual

[1] Lit. 'that I stay on'.

exercise of decoding the veiled speech of the poet's message. Sometimes, however, vagueness and obscurity reaches such a pitch that the average listener would be quite perplexed were it not for the fact that there is a tacit poetic convention to help him. Thus, it is assumed by both the reciter and his audience that every poem has a purpose when it is composed. There is hardly ever any hesitation in the mind of a Somali, when he is asked about the purpose of a particular poem. As we have said, Somali poetry serves as a medium of publicizing the poet's views, thoughts, and attitudes. It may be used for giving moral support to someone, or for undermining his prestige; it may be used as an instrument of war, or of peace and reconciliation. Even in poems concerned with love, especially the longer ones, there is often the utilitarian element of pleasing the clan of the woman to whom the poem is addressed, and securing some advantage in clan politics. Not infrequently, a man may publicize his reasons for a divorce or his dissatisfaction with an unhappy match, so as to defend himself against accusations of injustice.

Fables and stories are very seldom recited in poetic form and if they are, they are used only as allegories or allusions subordinated to the main theme and the main purpose of the poem.

Even when a poem is recited some time after it was composed, the original circumstances are usually remembered, and they provide the key to the meaning of obscure passages. If a reciter suspects that his audience is not familiar with this vital background information he takes the trouble to describe it to them in some detail before he begins to recite.

A Somali poet and his audience have a great appreciation of the beauty of nature and an intense interest in human emotions, but they would seldom consider describing them for their own sake. If a poem like Shelley's 'Ode to the West Wind' were translated into Somali alliterative verse and chanted to a Somali audience, they would wait till the end and then would inevitably ask, 'In what circumstances did the poet first recite the poem and what was his purpose?'

III · ORAL TRANSMISSION

A good poet usually has an entourage of admirers, some of whom learn by heart his poems and recite them wherever they go. It is from these admirers that other reciters learn the poems, if they consider them sufficiently beautiful and important to memorize. As there are many poets among the Somali, the competition for the ear of the public and the attention of the reciters is very keen. Criticism and scorn, accorded to poor or mediocre poetry, are merciless and readily condemn a poem to a death of silence and oblivion. Aware of this, most poets, except for a few of real genius, do not put their trust in improvisation, but spend many hours, sometimes even days, composing their works.

While we may admire Somali poets for achieving worthwhile results in the very difficult medium of Somali prosody, we are no less impressed by feats of memory on the part of the poetry reciters, some of whom are poets themselves. Unaided by writing they learn long poems by heart and some have repertoires which are too great to be exhausted even by several evenings of continuous recitation. Moreover, some of them are endowed with such powers of memory that they can learn a poem by heart after hearing it only once, which is quite astonishing, even allowing for the fact that poems are chanted very slowly, and important lines are sometimes repeated. The reciters are not only capable of acquiring a wide repertoire but can store it in their memories for many years, sometimes for their lifetime. We have met poets who at a ripe age could still remember many poems which they learnt in their early youth.

In the nomadic interior whole villages move from place to place and there is constant traffic between villages, grazing camps, and towns. Poems spread very quickly over wide areas and in recent times motor transport and the radio have further accelerated the speed with which they are disseminated.

A poem passes from mouth to mouth. Between a young Somali who listens today to a poem composed fifty years ago, five hundred miles away, and its first audience there is a long chain of reciters who passed it one to another. It is only natural that in this process of transmission some distortion occurs, but comparison of different versions of the same poem usually shows a surprisingly high degree of fidelity to the original. This is due to a large extent to the formal rigidity of Somali poetry: if one word is substituted for another, for instance, it must still keep to the rules of alliteration, thus limiting very considerably the number of possible changes. The general trend of the poem, on the other hand, inhibits the omission or transposition of lines.

Another factor also plays an important role: the audience who listen to the poem would soon detect any gross departure from the style of the particular poet; moreover, among the audience there are often people who already know by heart the particular poem, having learnt it from another source. Heated disputes sometimes arise between a reciter and his audience concerning the purity of his version. It may even happen that the authorship of a poem is questioned by the audience, who carefully listen to the introductory phrases in which the reciter gives the name of the poet, and, if he is dead, says a prayer formula for his soul.

Careful comparison of different versions of poems and the establishing of authoritative texts are tasks which await students of Somali. In this book we have decided not to go into details of this kind, as being beyond its scope. When other collections of poems are published, it will be interesting to compare the differences in the texts of the same poem. Although great care has been taken in obtaining reliable versions, we make no claim that the texts given in this book should be considered as authoritative.

IV · THE CLASSIFICATION OF SOMALI POEMS

The Somali classify their poems into various distinct types, each of which has its own specific name. It seems that their classification is mainly based on two prosodic factors: the type of tune to which the poem is chanted or sung, and the rhythmic pattern of the words.

Although both poet and audience are very much alive to the standards of correctness required for each type of poem, we have not met even one Somali who could state them explicitly. Yet these standards are universally accepted and there is seldom any difference of opinion as to whether a particular passage is correct or not.

In our researches we have been seriously handicapped by the lack of any study of the melodic and rhythmic features of Somali poetry by a competent musicologist. Unaided by such data, we have not been able to establish the nature of the units of which the rhythmic patterns are composed, and we have not succeeded in arriving at any definite formulations in this sphere. Our study of the number and length of syllables in each line and the distribution of accentual patterns among them has so far yielded very limited and disappointing results.

In addition to their distinctive prosodic features, types of Somali poems are further differentiated by their average length, their diction and style, and their range of subject matter; and while some poems are accompanied by hand-clapping or drumming, others are always recited without any accompaniment at all. In this sphere we have found that our observations were both easier to make and to verify than in that of Somali prosody.

Among Somali poems three types are regarded as most noble and best fitted for dealing with serious and important matters: the *gabay*, the *geeraar*, and the *jiifto*. Of the three the *gabay* is considered to be pre-eminent, and in fact the word '*gabay*' is sometimes used loosely as a general term for poetry. The *gabay*, the *jiifto*, and the *geeraar* are all composed as conscious and studied works of poetic art which, if well received, win lasting fame for their authors.

The 'gabay'

The *gabay* usually consists of between 30 and 150 lines, though shorter ones and considerably longer ones are not unknown. The number of syllables in each line varies from 14 to 18, and in the majority of cases there is a caesura before the sixth syllable from the end. In the nomadic interior the *gabay* is never recited with an accompaniment of music, drums, stepping, or clapping: there is in fact no participation on the part of the audience except for the occasional sporadic repetition of a particular line, hemistich, or word as a sign of delight and appreciation. A *gabay* accompanied by music can sometimes be heard on the radio, but this is an innovation which began in Mogadishu, under foreign influence.

The chant of the *gabay* usually has a simple melody with great variations in the length of notes. Some are held for a considerable time, and this applies particularly to those which correspond to the end of a line in the poem: in this position they fade gradually into silence. The tempo of the chant is slow and majestic, seldom changing throughout the poem. All emotional appeal depends on the expressive power of the words, and the reciter does not especially modulate his voice or accentuate any words or lines, thus giving an impression of superb restraint and stylization.

Although there is no definite restriction on the range of its subject matter, the *gabay* tends to deal mainly with serious themes, and any departure into humour and lightheartedness is usually of a satirical nature. The diction is characterized by a philosophical mood, with general observations about life interspersed throughout the poem. This slows down its movement and creates the impression of a gradual and stately unfolding of the poetic message. The *gabay* is often chanted at meetings and assemblies, and has recently become an important weapon of political propaganda. It is a major asset for a political party to have a good *gabay* composer on their side: the public will listen to him for the pleasure of it, even if they do not agree with his views.

In our collection the *gabay* is represented by the following poems: *The respect due to power; Poet's lament on the death of his wife; Ḥiin Finiin, the poet's favourite horse; The death of Richard Corfield; The road to damnation; The path of righteousness; A message to the Ogaadeen; An elder's reproof to his wife; The rewards of success; The looted necklace; The unpaid bridewealth;* and *Ingratitude.*

The 'jiifto'

The *jiifto* tends to be of the same length as the *gabay*, if not shorter. The average line consists of between 11 and 16 syllables, divided towards the middle by a caesura.

This form has always been less popular than the *gabay* and the *geeraar*: it reached its peak in the poetry of Sayyid Maḥammed ʿAbdille Ḥasan, and seems to be going out of fashion now. However, it shares many characteristics with the *gabay*: it is never, for instance, accompanied by music or chorus, and the chant is somewhat reminiscent of, but rather quicker than, that of the *gabay*. The *jiifto* also treats only serious subjects, those which tend to be particularly connected with melancholy and reflective moods, and it has sometimes been used as a vehicle of reproach or admonition.

In our collection the *jiifto* is represented by *The Sayyid's reply.*

The 'geeraar'

The *geeraar* is usually shorter than the *gabay*, and the number of syllables in the line usually varies between 6 and 8. This form also is always unaccompanied, and the chant is swifter and the melody livelier than in the *gabay*. Traditionally, the *geeraar* used to be recited on horseback, but this practice has been almost completely abandoned.

War and conflict is the usual subject matter of the *geeraar*, and it is said that in the old days, when one clan declared war on another, the challenge to fight at an appointed place was usually delivered in this form. It was also chanted to pour insults and abuse on one's opponents before the battle, and to raise the morale of one's own warriors.

The style is less elaborate and reflective than in the *gabay*, and in it can always be detected a note of urgency and rapid movement.

The *geeraar* is represented in this collection by *Oh clansmen, stop the war* and *The limits of submission*.

The 'buraambur'

The place of the *buraambur* is somewhere between the three 'classical' types already described, and the lighter and less elaborate poems. It tends to be shorter than the *gabay*, and has lines of between 14 and 16 syllables, with a caesura towards the middle of the line. It is occasionally accompanied by hand-clapping, stepping, drumming, or chorus.

Although the range of the subject-matter resembles that of the *gabay*, most *buraamburs* have a lighter touch, with less stylization and restraint in the actual recital. But the greatest difference lies in the fact that the *buraambur* is a poem composed by women for women—although men have been known to make interested listeners.

Examples of the *buraambur* in this collection are *A bridal song*, *Lament for a dead lover*, and *A woman sings of her love.*

The 'heello'

The structure of the *heello* is of quite a different nature from that of the types already discussed, although like them it is composed as a conscious and studied artistic activity and its authorship is usually known to the listeners. In form, however, it is a sequence of short poems (usually of only two lines), each of them constituting an independent unit.

It is usually performed before a large audience, who clap or stamp the rhythm and sometimes sing the chorus: it may also be accompanied by the lute and the tambourine and, more rarely, the flute. The separate elements of a *heello* sequence may be sung by different reciters, and the only feature which gives a sense of unity is the subject-matter, which is almost invariably love, the only departures being into the sphere of politics. There is a number of tunes to which the *heello* is sung, all of them lively.

There is much elaboration in the treatment of the subject, and allegory and metaphor are worked into a close-knit artistic form. As each part of the *heello* is so short, the poet, if he is to achieve an effect, often has to condense his message by encoding it into symbols. Thus, when the poet says

> Like a sailing ship caught in a typhoon
> I set my compass towards a desolate land,

his listeners understand that he is lamenting some misfortune, the desolate land symbolizing the absence of his beloved, and the ship tossed in a typhoon his own turbulent feelings.

The *heello* is usually recited as a form of light entertainment, not unlike 'pop' songs in the Western world. It is naturally very popular with the young, and with those who, though no longer young, are bent on the pursuit of the pleasures of carefree youth. Its hedonistic and ecstatic treatment of love has brought it into disrepute among the pious and the elderly. Although it often reaches a high poetic level, the *heello* is ephemeral, and new ones constantly rise to the zenith of popularity only to fade into oblivion within a few months. Unlike the poems of the classical tradition, even the best *heello* is soon forgotten.

While the origins of other types of poems go far back into the past, the *heello* is an innovation which was first introduced in 1945. Its creator, ʿAbdi Deeqsi, nicknamed 'Cinema', was the owner and driver of a trading lorry, and composed the first *heello* when his lorry broke down near Zeila. In a desolate place he sang his love song, beating the rhythm on an empty petrol tin. He called this type of poem *balwo* which is an Arabic borrowing and means in Somali 'evil' or 'misfortune'. The *balwo* soon became popular everywhere, and with the development of broadcasting it became an important feature of all radio programmes, often being provided with elaborate instrumental and choral accompaniments. Initially the only obstacle in its way to almost universal acceptance was its name, which deterred both the pious and the superstitious. Around 1950 it gradually came to be called *heello* instead, a neologism suggested by the meaningless words *heelloy*, *heellelooy*, which are usually sung before reciting the actual poems.

The *heello* is represented in this book by a sequence of poems under the title *Twelve modern love songs.*

The modern 'hees'.

Although the word *hees* means any kind of song, it is now often applied to a type of modern song which makes much use of political themes. Used very much in broadcasting, the *hees* is often highly topical, but like the *heello* it is of an ephemeral nature. In form the whole poem is continuous and not just an aggregate of separate verses: as it aims at reaching the widest possible public, its diction is simple and direct, without much allegory or complicated metaphors. The lively tunes to which it is sung often show the strong influence of European, or Europeanized Arabic music.

The modern *hees* can be regarded as the popular poetry of the modern urban community, with its strong political awareness. It is represented in our collection by the poem *Independence Song.*

Dance and work songs

The remaining types of poems are chiefly traditional dance and work songs: among the former we find also possession songs (*baahilaawe*), which are sung during dances inducing ecstatic and trancelike states.[1] The work songs are sung on all sorts of occasions, for instance by men when watering camels and by women while weaving mats.

The words of these songs are simple and lack the imagery found in the 'classical' poems, while the lines vary greatly in length and are few in number. Their authorship is seldom known, and most of them appear to be of considerable antiquity.

[1] See I. M. Lewis, *A Pastoral Democracy*, O.U.P. 1961, pp. 261 ff.

The dance songs are usually accompanied, quite apart from the dance movements themselves, by drumming and by clapping and stepping on the part of the audience; in certain types the women also ululate. Instrumental music is rare in the nomadic interior. Choral singing is used with both dance and work songs, and the melodies are lively, but not so elaborate as those of the *heello* and the *hees*.

These songs are represented in our collection by *Camel watering chant*, *Release*, *Choice*, *Fortitude*, *Dance hunger*, *A wish*, *The dancer's needs*, and *The best dance*.

V · SOMALI POETRY IN ARABIC

Arabic, as the language of Islam, has an important place in Somali life. In every nomadic village children learn the Quran in Arabic, and most of the prayers, both private and public, are said in Arabic. Students of Muslim Law and Theology have to reach a high standard of knowledge of this language to be able to read their textbooks. Men of religion constantly consult Arabic works when they prepare their sermons or make decisions in matters of law or conscience brought to them.

Among the educated *élite*, fully literate in Arabic, poets have turned their talents to the sacred language. As Arabic seems to the Somali people always particularly appropriate in the context of religious thought and worship, it is only natural that most of the poets using this language as their artistic medium have composed hymns or didactic poems. Arabic hymns are known by heart by many people and in fact religious literature in Arabic occupies a central position in the Somali culture. In view of this we have considered it essential to include in our present collection three examples of Arabic works by Somali poets. They are characteristic of Somalo-Arabic religious poetry and are composed in the classical tradition, with only some slight deviations occasioned by the Somali background. The manuscripts of the Arabic poems given in our collection have all been written fairly recently, within the present century. They contain some imperfections and we are aware of the possibility of alternative interpretations of obscure passages, but we have decided not to go into detailed discussions of possible variant readings, leaving this task to such Arabists as may perhaps be attracted by this very rich field. Instead of printing the three poems we have provided photocopies, a measure which has the advantage of showing the interested reader the type of Arabic calligraphy employed, and of relieving us from the heavy responsibility of editing the text.

It may be of interest to note that some Somali poets have acquired fame through their works both in Somali and Arabic. Among them, Sayyid Maḥammed ʿAbdille Ḥasan is an outstanding example of this poetic bilingualism.

VI · BIOGRAPHICAL NOTES

In view of the position which poetry occupies in Somali culture, it is not surprising that the lives and activities of well-known Somali poets should be of general interest. In what follows we present such bibliographical information as we have been able to obtain on the main poets whose works are represented in this collection.

Sayyid Maḥammed ʿAbdille Ḥasan

There is no doubt that the most outstanding figure among them is Maḥammed ʿAbdille Ḥasan. He was born on 7 April 1864[1] at a small watering place between Wudwud (Wiḍwiḍ) and Bohotle (Buuhodle) in the Ḍulbahante country of the eastern part of the former British Somaliland Protectorate. His grandfather, Sheikh Ḥasan Nuur, of the Bah Geri section of the Ogaadeen clan, had settled amongst the Ḍulbahante in 1826 and had married locally, one of his sons being Maḥammed's father. At the age of seven, Maḥammed began to learn the Quran under a local teacher, and by the age of ten when his grandfather died, he could read the Quran and became his teacher's assistant. Five years later, he set up as a teacher of religion on his own account, and by the early age of nineteen he had won the title 'sheikh' for his learning.

About this time, he left his home to travel widely in search of further learning, and visited such local seats of Islam as Harar and Mogadishu, as well as the distant Sudan and Nairobi. Some nine years were spent thus. About 1891 he returned to the

[1] This date and much other material are based on information from Sheikh Maḥammed's son, Sheikh ʿAbdurraḥmaan Sheikh Maḥammed, and his brother, Sheikh Ḥasan Sheikh ʿAbdille, and others who were closely associated with the movement.

Ḍulbahante country and married a woman of the Ogaadeen clan. Three years later he set out in company with thirteen other sheikhs to go on pilgrimage to Mecca, and spent about a year abroad travelling as far as Hejaz and Palestine. While at Mecca, Sheikh Maḥammed met Sayyid Muḥammad Ṣaaliḥ and joined his Religious Order, the Ṣaaliḥiya.[1] When he returned to Somaliland he settled for a time at Berbera where, with messianic zeal, he preached the reformist doctrine of his Order. He condemned smoking, the chewing of the stimulant leaves of the qat (*qaad*) plant,[2] and generally denounced excessive indulgence and luxuries, calling on people to return to the strict path of Muslim puritanism.

Sheikh Maḥammed's religious campaign for the new Saaliḥiya Order naturally attracted considerable attention, and not a little opposition, especially on the part of the strongly established Qaadiriya Order. This, however, only served to increase his fervour and he soon adopted the slogan that the Qaadiriya were 'dead', whereas the Saaliḥiya were alive, since their founder Sayyid Muḥammad Ṣaaliḥ, was alive and active at Mecca, while the Qaadiriya founder, Sayyid ʿAbdul Qaadir[3] al-Jiilaani had died in the twelfth century. But what appears to have fired Sheikh Maḥammed ʿAbdille's patriotism and stimulated his xenophobic passion was the activities of the French Roman Catholic mission near Berbera. Certainly the conversion of Somali children to Christianity, and their adoption of Christian names, left a deep imprint upon his mind, and convinced him that the ultimate aim of Christian colonization was the destruction of his country's religion.

Initially, however, Sheikh Maḥammed's campaign met with relatively little success on the coast, and in 1897 he retired to his home amongst the Ḍulbahante where he built a mosque and opened a teaching settlement for his Order. Here he intensified his denunciation of the Christian colonizers, although ostensibly co-operating with the government at Berbera, and consolidated his influence by successfully intervening as a mediator in clan disputes. In 1899 the incident occurred in which he was alleged by the local administration to have stolen a rifle and this was

[1] In Somali the name of this Order is pronounced with an initial *s* instead of with the Arabic *ṣ*.

[2] *Catha aedulis.*

[3] This name is often transliterated as ʿAbd al-Ḳādir or ʿAbdu -l-Qādir.

followed by a hostile exchange of messages. Thereafter events developed with amazing rapidity, and within the year Sheikh Maḥammed had proclaimed a holy war against the 'infidel' colonizers and was in turn declared a rebel by the Berbera government. The long-drawn-out war which followed has already been described and requires no further comment here. It effectively ended with the bombing of the Sheikh's stronghold at Taleh (Taleeḥ) in February 1920, and although Sheikh Maḥammed himself survived the engagements which followed this, he died shortly afterwards, probably of influenza or malaria, at Guano Imi in Ethiopia on 21 December 1920. Thus, in the words of a recent Somali chronicler of the rebellion, 'ended the life of the man who had fought great odds'. He was only fifty-six years of age when he died, and although he had in the course of his life contracted more than a dozen marriages, he was survived by only nine sons and one daughter.

Sheikh Maḥammed is said to have left a number of Arabic manuscript works on religious themes, but it is chiefly for his Somali poetry that he is remembered. For him poetry was often a political device and many of his poems were originally recited directly to his immediate entourage and thereafter memorized by his court recorders who broadcast his words throughout the country.

While he did not succeed in his stated object of driving the 'infidels' who had seized his country into the sea, and despite his tyrannical rule and his savage punishments, he is universally regarded as one of the greatest figures of recent Somali history and as one of the founders of modern Somali nationalism. And indeed as Jardine, the author of the official history of the period, correctly judged forty years ago, 'In the hearts of his countrymen . . . he will live for ever as a national hero. . . .'[1] Yet it is not so much by the title 'Sayyid', which he assumed to lead his followers, that he is remembered today, but rather by the much more familiar name 'son of 'Abdille Ḥasan'. And this is perhaps an indication of how vividly the memory of this remarkable man still persists, in the forefront of the Somali

[1] D. Jardine, *The Mad Mullah of Somaliland*, 1923, p. 308. This history of the campaigns against the Dervishes, written by the Chief Secretary to the Somaliland Government at the time, gives a very full picture of the period. But in matters of detail regarding Sheikh Maḥammed's life it is not always accurate.

national consciousness, not merely as a symbol, but also as a reminder of a truly outstanding personality exemplifying the most cherished Somali ideals of daring, independence, and dauntless panache.

Ismaaʿiil Mire

This poet, born in 1884, was a close associate of Sheikh Maḥammed ʿAbdille Ḥasan and acted as one of his advisers and battle leaders. He led the Dervish attack on the Camel Constabulary in the battle of Ḍul Madoobe on 9 August 1913. He died about 1950.

He belonged to the ʿAli Geri section of the Ḍulbahante clan and was thus a maternal relative of Sheikh Maḥammed; it was among his own clansmen that he first attracted attention as a skilful leader of great courage and prudence. This training served him well when he embraced the Dervish cause. He remained faithful to Sheikh Maḥammed to the end and survived the defeat of the Dervishes and the bitterness and desolation which followed. To some extent this experience seems to be reflected in his later work, as for example in his *Rewards of success*. Above all he is remembered as an authority on Somali history and custom. Many of his poems immortalize the history of his times and constitute an important source for the recent history of Northern Somaliland.

Faaraḥ Nuur

Another poet of much the same period, who died about 1930, is Faaraḥ Nuur of the Arab[1] clan, a section of the Isaaq. Faaraḥ played an important part in emancipating his people from their bondage to the strong ʿIidegale clan with which they had a long-standing association. Traditional accounts of the Arab rebellion confirm the trial of patience which eventually led to violent revolt, recorded in the poem *The limits of submission*. The poet is of particular interest, apparently, in being one of the few Somalis of his time who were aware of the far-reaching significance of the first moves in the imperial partition of his country. Thus in one of his poems the following comment was made and often repeated after him:

[1] This is a Somali clan, not to be confused with Arabs proper, who are called ʿArab, with the initial 'ain' sound as in Arabic.

1 *Ingriis, Amchaar iyo Talyaan* *way akeekami ye*
2 *Arlada yaa La kala boobayaa* *ka u itaal roon e*
3 *Waa duni La kala iibsaday* *aan naLa ogaysiin e*
4 *Anse la ah, Aakhiru Sabaan* *iligyadiisii ye*

1 The British, the Ethiopians, and the Italians are squabbling,
2 The country is snatched and divided by whosoever is stronger,
3 The country is sold piece by piece without our knowledge,
4 And for me, all this is the teeth of the last days of the world.

And to some the struggle of his clan for independence and their spectacular victory against overwhelming odds symbolized the wider movement of the Somali nation towards independence.

'Abdillaahi Muuse

This author of the Habar Yoonis clan was born towards the end of the last century and is still alive today. Unlike the preceding poets, 'Abdillaahi Muuse did not achieve fame as a war leader, but is on the contrary a man of peace, well known and respected for his piety and wisdom. Having memorized the whole Quran he has won the customary title 'The Keeper of the Quran'. Thus often in his verse the importance of goodwill and co-operation is stressed, as in the following lines in one of his poems, which have become proverbial:

1 *Is taageerid bay laba gacmood* *tamar ku yeeshaan e*
2 *Tiska wacha La qaadaa hadday* *tiirisaa bidich e*
3 *Hadday midigtu keli taagantahay* *tachar ma goyseen e*

1 It is in supporting one another that two hands find strength,
2 A thorny branch can only be carried, if the left hand is helping (the right one),
3 The right hand raised alone could not cut even a morsel of gristle.

Raage Ugaas

Like 'Abdillaahi Muuse, but living several generations earlier Raage Ugaas was also primarily a man of peace and a skilful arbitrator in clan affairs. The success which his patience and prudence achieved are still quoted as a model. These qualities and a certain strain of mellowness, even gentleness, combined with restrained command of imagery are reflected in much of his poetry. Raage Ugaas, the son of a sultan, belonged to the Ogaadeen clan, renowned for the purity of its Somali speech. One of the poet's greatest qualities was his masterful use of the resources of the language and his adherence to a classical style of Somali.

Salaan ʿArrabey

Salaan ʿArrabey, who was born about the middle of the nineteenth century and died in the early nineteen-forties, is generally regarded as one of the most versatile Somali poets, and while Raage Ugaas represents the traditional Somali outlook on life, Salaan ʿArrabey was in many ways an innovator, both in the themes he treated in his verse and in his choice and use of language. He did not hesitate to use foreign borrowings and to invent words, drawing upon his knowledge of Arabic, English, Swahili, and Hindustani; for like many of his clansmen of the Habar Toljaʿlo he was an inveterate traveller and during his long life spent many years abroad in Aden and in East Africa, sometimes in trade, and on other occasions working as an interpreter and guide for foreigners. His contact with Europeans earned him a reputation as one skilful in dealing with foreign administrators. His business affairs appeared to have their ups and downs, as he was a man given to great generosity and reckless liberality. He was an emotional, and even passionate person, well known for his courage and his ebullient humour, given to spectacular practical jokes which are still remembered today.

The power of Salaan's poems was such that he was often credited with being equally able to inspire a clan war or peace, and indeed to his well-known poem 'Landmine' (*Mayn*), composed before the First World War, is attributed a serious outbreak of inter-clan violence in Burao Town.

Not only have numerous poems of his survived, but many of his sayings have become proverbial. Recently, some of his verse has been applied to further the cause of Somali nationalism, and in this context the following lines of the poem 'Landmine' are quoted:

1 *Haddaad dhimato mar bay geeridu nolosha dhaantaa ye*
2 *Dhaqashiyo mar bay Kaa yihiin dhereggu chaaraan e*

1 If you die, sometimes death is better than life (of shame),
2 Sometimes prosperity and repletion are degrading and vile.

SELECT BIBLIOGRAPHIES

I · THE SOCIAL AND CULTURAL SETTING

BURTON, R. F., 1894. *First Footsteps in Eastern Africa*, Memorial edition, two volumes, London.

CERULLI, E., 1957. *Somalia I. Scritti vari editi ed inediti*, Rome.

GOVERNMENT OF THE SOMALI REPUBLIC, 1962. *The Somali Peninsula: A New Light on Imperial Motives*, London.

*HUNT, J. A., 1951. *A General Survey of the Somaliland Protectorate, 1944–1950*, London.

JARDINE, D., 1923. *The Mad Mullah of Somaliland*, London.

LEWIS, I. M., 1955 and 1956. 'Sufism in Somaliland: A Study in Tribal Islam,' *Bulletin of the School of Oriental and African Studies*, xvii. 3, pp. 581–602; xviii. 1, pp. 146–60.

*—— 1960. 'The Somali Conquest of the Horn of Africa', *Journal of African History*, i. 2, pp. 213–30.

*—— 1961. *A Pastoral Democracy. A Study of Pastoralism and Politics among the Northern Somali of the Horn of Africa*, O.U.P., London.

—— 1962. *Marriage and the Family in Northern Somaliland*, London.

TRIMINGHAM, J. S., 1952. *Islam in Ethiopia*, O.U.P., London.

II · THE SOMALI LANGUAGE

ʿABDULLĀHI HHĀJI MAHHAMŪD and BRUNO PANZA, 1960. *Afkayaga Hōyo*, Edizioni Arte e Cultura, Mogadiscio.

ANDRZEJEWSKI, B. W., 1954. 'Some Problems of Somali Orthography', *The Somaliland Journal*, Hargeisa, pp. 34–47.

—— 1955. 'The Problem of Vowel Representation in the Isaaq Dialect of Somali', *Bulletin of the School of Oriental and African Studies*, xviii. 3, pp. 567–80.

—— 1961. 'Notes on the Substantive Pronouns in Somali', *African Language Studies*, II, London, pp. 80–99.

—— 1963. 'Speech and Writing Dichotomy as a Pattern of Multilingualism in the Somali Republic', *Report of the C.C.T.A./C.S.A. Symposium on Multilingualism in Africa*, Brazzaville, 1962 (in the press).

ARMSTRONG, LILIAS, E., 1934. 'The Phonetic Structure of Somali', *Mitteilungen des Seminars für Orientalische Sprachen zu Berlin*, xxxvii/iii, pp. 116–61.

BELL, C. R. V., 1953. *The Somali Language*, Longmans, London.

CERULLI, E., 1932. 'Tentativo indigeno di formare un alfabeto somalo', *Oriente Moderno*, xii, Rome, pp. 212–13.

* These works contain useful bibliographies from which this short list can be supplemented.

GALAAL, M. H. I., 1954. 'Arabic Script for Somali', *The Islamic Quarterly*, 1/2, London, pp. 114–18.

*—— 1956. *Ḥikmad Soomaali*, edited with grammatical introduction and notes by B. W. Andrzejewski, Annotated African Texts IV, School of Oriental and African Studies, Oxford University Press.

KING, J. S., 1887. 'Somali as a Written Language', *The Indian Antiquary*, Bombay, pp. 242–3 and pp. 285–7.

LEWIS, I. M., 1958. 'The Gadabuursi Somali Script', *Bulletin of the School of Oriental and African Studies*, xxi. 1, pp. 134–56.

MAINO, MARIO, 1951. 'Alfabeto "Osmania"', *Rassegna di Studi Etiopici*, x, pp. 108–21.

*—— 1953. *La lingua somala—-strumento d'insegnamento professionale*, Allessandria.

MORENO, M. M., 1955. *Il somalo della Somalia, grammatica e testi del Benadir, Darod e Dighil*, Rome, Istituto Poligrafico dello Stato.

TILING, MARIA VON, 1925. *Somali-Texte und Untersuchungen zur Somali Lautlehre*, Achtes Beiheft zur Zeitschrift fur Eingeborenen Sprachen, Berlin.

TUCKER, A. E. and BRYAN, M. A., 1956. *The non-Bantu Languages of North-East Africa*. Handbook of African Languages, Part III, International African Institute, Oxford University Press.

—— —— *Linguistic Analyses*, a supplement to the work quoted above (in the press).

*TUCKER, A. N., 1961. 'Problèmes de typologie dans la classification des langues non-bantu de l'Afrique du Nord-Est', *Journal de la Societé des Africanistes*, pp. 59–74.

III • CHARACTERISTICS OF SOMALI VERSE

BERGHOLD, K., 1899. 'Somali Studien', *Vienna Oriental Journal* (*Wiener Zeitschrift für die Kunde des Morgenlandes*), xiii, pp. 123–98.

DUCHENET, E., 1938. 'Le chant dans le folklore Somali', *Revue de Folklore Français*, ix, Avril–Juin, pp. 72–87.

KIRK, J. W. C., 1905. *A Grammar of the Somali Language*, Cambridge University Press.

LAURENCE, MARGARET, 1954. *A Tree for Poverty*, Nairobi, The Eagle Press.

MAINO, MARIO, 1953. *La lingua somala—-strumento d'insegnamento professionale*, Alessandria.

* These works contain useful bibliographies from which this short list can be supplemented.

PART TWO

THE POEMS

A · CLASSICAL POETRY

B · TRADITIONAL AND MODERN SONGS

C · RELIGIOUS POETRY IN ARABIC

A · CLASSICAL POETRY

1. *The Respect Due to Power*

RAAGE UGAAS

1 A forest with lions and a place where the buttocks and manes of beasts of prey are seen,
2 Can only be crossed by stilling all sound; leave them unroused.
3 If you catch your thumb in the thorny thickness of the fold-fence
4 You withdraw your hand carefully without shaking your whole arm.
5 He who stands above you on that day, and pays tribute to no one,
6 Must be answered softly and not with harsh words.

2. *Poet's Lament on the Death of his Wife*

RAAGE UGAAS

1 Like the *yuʿub*[1] wood bell tied to gelded camels that are running away,
2 Or like camels which are being separated from their young,
3 Or like people journeying while moving camp,
4 Or like a well which has broken its sides or a river which has overflowed its banks,
5 Or like an old woman whose only son was killed,
6 Or like the poor, dividing the scraps for their frugal meal,
7 Or like the bees entering their hive, or food crackling in the frying,
8 Yesterday my lamentations drove sleep from all the camps.
9 Have I been left bereft in my house and shelter?
10 Has the envy of others been miraculously fulfilled?

[1] *Gyrocarpus Asiaticus* Willd. (Peck). For details concerning Somali plants mentioned in this book, see P. E. Glover, *A Provisional Check-List of British and Italian Somaliland Trees, Shrubs and Herbs*, Crown Agents for the Colonies, London, 1947.

1 Sud libaach leh meel bahal salkiyo   saymo La arkayo

2 Sanqadh tirashadaa Lagu maraa   Laga ma soo saaro

3 Suryo oodan meeshii surdub ah   suul haddaad geliso

4 Qun yar baa siddaha Loo bachshaa   laanta La ma saydho

5 Ninkii maalintaa Kaa sita een   Laga sad qaadaynin

6 Sawd gibin ah baa Loo ceshaa   Lagu ma sooyaansho

1 Sida koorta yucub oo La suray   korommo buubaal ah

2 Ama geel ka reeb ah oo nirgaha   Laga kachaynaayo
3 Ama beelo kaynaan ah oo   kor u hayaamaaya
4 Ama ceel karkaarrada jebshiyo   webi karaar dhaafay

5 Ama habar kurkii wadnaha   Lagaga kaw siiyay
6 Ama kaal danley qaybsatiyo   kur iyo dhaal yaabis
7 Shinni kaaluf galay ama sidii   koronkorro oomi

8 Chalay kololo'aygii ma ladin   kaamil reeruhu e
9 Kunbulkiyo ardaagii miyaa   Laygu kaliyeeyay
10 Wichii Laygu kuunyeeyay miyaa   igu karaamoobay

11 Have I been deprived of the fried meat and reserves for lean times which were so plentiful for me?
12 Have I today been taken from the chessboard (of life)?
13 Have I been borne on a saddle to a distant and desolate place?
14 Have I broken my shin, a bone which cannot be mended?

3. *Ḥiin Finiin, the Poet's Favourite Horse*

MAḤAMMED ʿABDILLE ḤASAN

Ḥiin Finiin was the poet's favourite pony and, though small, the swiftest and finest among the Dervishes' horses. When, in the course of the holy war, Sheikh Maḥammed sought to make an alliance with the ʿUmar Maḥamuud lineage of the Majeerteen clan and to marry their leader's sister, this horse was requested as betrothal payment. By making this virtually impossible demand the girl's kinsmen hoped to evade the proposed alliance. But, after much heart-searching, Sheikh Maḥammed agreed to part with his treasured mount. The poem laments his loss.

1 Long life, Faaraḥ! Men are entitled to straightforward and respectful words,
2 And I am a respectful man except when I am slighted,
3 And friendship and openheartedness was my wont until the hateful envy of the infidels was unleashed upon me,
4 And you have come to me bearing a message which a man of authority has written.
5 Had you yourself sought from me countless wealth and livestock,
6 I would not have hesitated in meeting your request,
7 And indeed I intended to present you with a gift of fine camels from the herds
8 And I meant to order thousands of those fine beasts to be driven into a corral for you,
9 But when you decided upon Ḥiin Finiin[1] you made me heavy with pain.
10 Oh Beloved, certain desires make men culpable and call for punishment;

[1] *Ḥiin Finiin*, lit. 'the sound of gravel', referring to the noise made by a horse galloping over stony ground such as is common in Somaliland.

11 Kunbiskii miyaa Layga qubay   kolayo ii buuchay?

12 Maanta na kataantii miyaa   Layga kala qaaday?
13 Kob abaar ah oo dheche miyaa   koore ila meeray?

14 Kub miyaan ka jabay biichiyaan   kabayo Loo haynin?

1 Chayow Faarachow, hadal rag waa   Loo chutubiyaa ye

2 Nin chishoonayaan ahay haddaan   Lay chistiyahayn e
3 Chabiib baan ahaa jeer kufriga   Laygu chaasiday e

4 Adna chaashad baad ila timid   chaakin soo qoray e

5 Chaddigii adduunyo iyo haddaad   choolo iga dooni

6 Kolla anigu Kaa ma chayireen   chaal aad leedahay e
7 Inaan Kuu chaf gooyaan jeclaa   geel chawaad badan e

8 Kumanyaal chawaad aan lahaa   chawdh u sii mari ye

9 Markaad se Chiin Finiin damacday baan   Kaa chanuunsaday e
10 Waar, maandhow, chirgiga qaarki waa   Lagu chujoobaa ye

11 But I am mild and respectful because we are relatives,
12 And however ungenerous my conduct to others, to you I am kind.
13 If other kinsmen near or distant, or relatives by marriage, had asked me,
14 Even if I had been coaxed with the mention of the Living One and the Self-Existing One,[1]
15 I would not have it in my heart to give them Ḥiisow,[2] the beautiful one,
16 And he is bay; for in colour horses are not equal.
17 The gallop, the trot, the canter, the walk,
18 To whichever you turn him he is without equal.
19 Oh, you the straight-limbed one; this beast is without peer;
20 And whenever he comes into my thoughts my love for him is re-kindled,
21 And nothing except the letter of my faith surpasses my love for him.
22 To mount him with might for the holy war was my desire,
23 On his back I would have claimed the rights of which I was deprived;
24 It was upon him that I intended to make a feast of my enemies for the hornbill,[3] (the witness of death),
25 On him in the Ḥays[4] rains I intended to attack from Ḥalin,
26 And between there and the coast to loot camels,
27 And on his back I meant to cut off the testicles of the menstruating infidels.
28 Until I had driven long spears through the shameless Reer Hagar,[5]
29 And until the shedding of their thick blood had been celebrated with rejoicing,
30 And until they had been massacred and destroyed utterly,

[1] The 'Living One' and the 'Self-Existing One' are names of God in Islamic doctrine; for further information about the use of these names see I. M. Lewis, 'The Names of God in Northern Somali', *Bulletin of the School of Oriental and African Studies*, xxii. 1 (1959), pp. 134–40.

[2] *Ḥiisow*, another praise name for *Ḥiin Finiin*; the etymology of the word suggests 'beauty'.

[3] The hornbill is connected with death and for Somali has macabre associations.

[4] A short rain season usually falling between December and January.

[5] A prominent lineage of the Ḍulbahante clan which had failed to support the Sayyid and his followers.

11 Wachaan Kuu chutubiyaa ba waa   chuuradaan nahay e
12 Nin kalaan chafiilo ba adaan   chayda Kaa rogay e

13 Chigto iyo qaraabiyo hadduu   chidid i weydiisto

14 Chayi iyo Qayuum haddii   La igu choodaansho

15 Chubbigayga ku ma hayn inaan   Chiisow bichiyaa ye

16 Chamar weeye oo midab fardood   kala chariir roon e
17 Chawaare iyo kadlo iyo jeefag iyo   chawle iyo koose
18 Chaggii Loo rogo ba waa gammaan   chulashadiisii ye
19 Chubnatoosanlow, neefku waa   chaalad gooni yah e

20 Goortaan chusuus ula noqduu   chiise i qaban e

21 Wachaan charafka diimeed ahayn   igaga cheel dheer e

22 Charbiga iyo jahaadkaan lahaa   choogsi ugu fuul e
23 Chaqaygii maqnaa baan lahaa   chag ugu raacdee ye

24 Isagaan chateeyada lahaa   chuurta ugu loog e

25 Chayska da'ayaan lahaa   Chalin ka dooyee ye
26 Meesha iyo cheebtaan lahaa   Chiito ka eryood e
27 Chiniinyaha ku goo baan lahaa   gaalka chaylka leh e

28 Chujooyi reebta Reer Hagar anaan   chamashyadii ruubin

29 Chinjirtooda dhiigga ah haddaan   Lagu charaaraysan

30 Chaaqaamaquuqa iyo haddaan   chaaluf Laga yeelin

31 And until my task had been fulfilled, I would not have given up Ḥiddaysane.[1]
32 But always in the world there are evil-doers skulking,
33 They spread slander like the Ethiopian Isaaq,[2]
34 And I fear that they will spoil my reputation;
35 And alas, to a man of honour slander is ever shameful,
36 And as a pilgrim I cannot in these times afford miserliness;
37 Instead of being talked about behind my back, I am now free from blame; the sense of obligation has shifted away from me.
38 The fine bay horse this evening is among your herds.
39. It is Ḥiin Finiin that you hold on a rope,
40 And all the other beasts shy away from him with reverence.
41 Since the Sultan to whom I owe respect has insisted on having it,
42 Take its bridle; I would not have honoured another man with it!

4. *The Death of Richard Corfield*

MAḤAMMED ʿABDILLE ḤASAN

This poem was composed to celebrate the death of Richard Corfield in the battle of Dul Madoba (Ḍul Madoobe) on 9 August 1913, when a large party of the Dervishes surrounded and launched a fierce attack against the camel detachment which Corfield commanded. Corfield had been sent to Somaliland to organize a camel constabulary to restore some order out of the chaos which had followed the ill-fated policy of coastal concentration pursued by the British Government between 1910 and 1912. His field of action was, however, firmly restricted to protecting the main clans friendly to the British within a limited area. He was to avoid engagements with the Dervishes as far as possible. But Corfield was a man of courage and determination and in the events which led to his death at Dul Madoba disregarded his orders.[3] In the battle he was struck in the head by a Dervish bullet and apparently died instantly. Consequently, the savage manner of his death described exultantly by the poet seems to be exaggerated.

[1] Another praise name for *Ḥiin Finiin*; the etymology is obscure.

[2] This is a reference to the derivation of a large fraction of the Isaaq peoples from an Ethiopian woman on their maternal side. Here it is used disparagingly since the Dervishes were at war with the Ethiopians and also with many of the Isaaq.

[3] For an account of Corfield's career in Somaliland see H. F. Prevost Battersby, *Richard Corfield of Somaliland*, London, 1914.

31 Chiddaysane ma dhiibeen e anaan   chaajaday bogan e

32 Charaami uun baa arlada   chula abiidkiis e
33 Wuchuun bay chushleeyaan sidii   Chabasha Iidoor e
34 Anigu na chogtaydaan ka biqi   inay chumeeyaan e
35 Chaasha Lillaahi e nin gob ah   chamasho waw ceeb e
36 Goorteer anoo chaaji yaan   chinif awoodayn e
37 Intii aniga Lay chaman lahaa   chil iga soo meeri

38 Adiguu galabta Kuu choolo yahay   chamarkii dheeraa ye
39 Waa Chiin Finiin neefka aad   chadhigga haysaa ye
40 Chayawaanka oo idil naftay   kala cheraadaan e
41 Mar hadduu suldaan igu chil lihi   igaga chaydaantay

42 Chadhigiisa qabo aadmi kale   kuma churmeeyeen e!

The poem was composed by Sheikh Maḥammed shortly after the news of the battle was reported to him.

Stylistically, it will be seen that many of the lines in the poem are set in the form of injunctions introduced by the word 'say', in a manner reminiscent of the diction of the Quran.

This poem reappeared as recently as 1959 in a political broadsheet distributed in Mogadishu.

1 You have died, Corfield, and are no longer in this world,
2 A merciless journey was your portion.
3 When, Hell-destined, you set out for the Other World
4 Those who have gone to Heaven will question you, if God is willing;
5 When you see the companions of the faithful and the jewels of Heaven,
6 Answer them how God tried you.
7 Say to them: 'From that day to this the Dervishes never ceased their assaults upon us.
8 The British were broken, the noise of battle engulfed us;
9 With fervour and faith the Dervishes attacked us.'
10 Say: 'They attacked us at mid-morning.'
11 Say: 'Yesterday in the holy war a bullet from one of their old rifles struck me.
12 And the bullet struck me in the arm.'
13 Say: 'In fury they fell upon us.'
14 Report how savagely their swords tore you,
15 Show these past generations in how many places the daggers were plunged.
16 Say: '"Friend," I called, "have compassion and spare me!"'
17 Say: 'As I looked fearfully from side to side my heart was plucked from its sheath.'
18 Say: 'My eyes stiffened as I watched with horror;
19 The mercy I implored was not granted.'
20 Say: 'Striking with spear-butts at my mouth they silenced my soft words;
21 My ears, straining for deliverance, found nothing;
22 The risk I took, the mistake I made, cost my life.'
23 Say: 'Like the war leaders of old, I cherished great plans for victory.'
24 Say: 'The schemes the djinns planted in me brought my ruin.'
25 Say: 'When pain racked me everywhere

1 Adaa jiitayaan, Koofiyow,   dunida joogayn e
2 Adigaa jidkii LaGugu wacay   jimicla'aaneed e
3 Jahannamo-La-geeyow, haddaad   Aakhirow jahato
4 Nimankii Janno u kacay war bay   jerin inshaalleeye

5 Jameecooyinkii iyo haddaad   jawhartii aragto

6 Sida Eebbahay Kuu jirrabay   mari jawaabteeda
7 Daraawiish jigraar naga ma deyn   tan iyo jeerkii dheh

8 Ingriis jab yoo wacha ku dhacay   jac iyo baaruud e
9 Wachay noo jajuunteen na waa   jibasho diineed dheh
10 Jigta weerar bay goor barqo ah   nagu jiteeyeen dheh
11 Aniga jikray ila heleen   shalay jahaadkii dheh

12 Jeeniga hortiisay rasaas   igaga joojeen dheh
13 Jiiraayaday ila dheceen   jiricafkoodii dheh
14 Siday Kuugu jeecheen magliga   jararacdii sheego
15 Billaawuhu siduu Kuu jarjaray   jeerarka u muuji

16 Naf jaclaysigeed baan u iri   jaalow iga daa dheh
17 Jaljalleecadii baa wadnaha   jeeb ka soo ruqay dheh

18 Jeedaaladii baa indhuhu   kor u jillaadmeen dheh
19 Jimic ka ma helin tuugmadaan   jeriyay ruuchii dheh
20 Kolkaan juuq iraahdo ba afkay   iga jifeeyeen dheh

21 Wach badan baan jalleecee dhegaan   jalaq La ii siinin
22 Goortaan jarreero na gafoo   nolol ka jaan qaaday
23 Sida janannadii hore tashigu   igu jaguugnaa dheh

24 Taladii jinnigu ii hor maray   jaasadeed helay dheh

25 Jiidaha chanuunka leh markii   La igu jeeraarshay

26 Men lay sleepless at my shrieks.'
27 Say: 'Great shouts acclaimed the departing of my soul.'
28 Say: 'Beasts of prey have eaten my flesh and torn it apart for meat.'
29 Say: 'The sound of swallowing the flesh and the fat comes from the hyena.'
30 Say: 'The crows plucked out my veins and tendons.'
31 Say: 'If stubborn denials are to be abandoned, then my clansmen were defeated.'
32 In the last stand of resistance there is always great slaughter.
33 Say: 'The Dervishes are like the advancing thunderbolts of a storm, rumbling and roaring.'

5. *The Sayyid's Reply*

MAḤAMMED ʿABDILLE ḤASAN

Throughout his long struggle with the British and their allies Sheikh Maḥammed kept up a spirited exchange of letters and verbal messages with all his enemies. Often his words were then broadcast through the medium of poetry, as in the case of the present poem, when the Sayyid judged such publicity to be in the Dervish interest and inimical to his foes. Here, in the style of a defendant stating his case before a Somali court of arbitration, the poet neatly counters each charge made against him in a message from the British. As well as being of interest for the skill with which Sheikh Maḥammed turns each charge made against him into an attack upon his accusers, the poem reveals how the nationalist leader regarded the Italian colonizers of Somalia. These, not without justice, the Sayyid sees as having been brought to his country by the British and encouraged to join the fight against him. But above all this poem reveals Sheikh Maḥammed's consummate command of invective, ridicule, and scorn, of which by any literary standards he must be judged to be a master.

1 Concerning your plea 'Do not incite the Ogaadeen against us' I also have a complaint.
2 The people of the Ethiopian region[1] look for nothing from you,
3 So do not press my claim against them.
4 Do not claim on my behalf the blood money which they owe me.
5 I will myself seek to recover the property and the loot which they have seized.
6 Were I to leave a single penny with them my pledge would be perverted.

[1] Mainly of the Ogaadeen clan.

26 Jibaadka iga soo bachay dadkii   jiifka qaban waa dheh
27 Kolkay rubaddu jow tiri or bay   iga ag jiibsheen dheh
28 Jiirkaygii na bahal baa cunoo   jiitay hilibkii dheh

29 Jurmidiyo baruurtii dhurwaa   juguch ka siiyaa dheh

30 Jiiljiiladiyo seedahay tukuu   igaga jaadeen dheh
31 Haddaan Lays jikaarayn tolkay   Laga jiilroonaa dheh

32 Weligood wacha Lagu jaraa   jilibdhig duulaan dheh
33 Daraawiishi waa jibin dhowga iyo   jowga soo bichi dheh.

1 Ogaadeen ha ii dirin   dacwad baan ka leeyahay

2 War, duul haad Amchaaraha   adiga Kaa ma dayayee
3 Deyntaan ku leeyahay   dun ha iiga qaadin e
4 Wuchuu aniga iga dilo   diyo hayga siinin e

5 Amba waa ka dabo geli   dakankiyo qaadkee

6 Dirham haddii aan kaga tago   anaa been dabaad ah e

7 What I claim from you is only what you yourself owe me;
8 Since you are the government the responsibility is yours,
9 Can you disclaim those whom you tricked into attacking me?
10 Do they not swim in the prosperity which they have gained from what they devoured of mine?
11 Do they not drive their livestock from the valley of ʿAado to the west?
12 What did they seek from the lands between Burao and your stations?
13 Had you a pact with them by God and by consent?
14 Or did thirst drive them mad? Fools easily lose their way.
15 And afterwards was it not into your pockets that you poured the wealth?
16 Did you not enter the amounts of the booty in your printed books and cash ledgers?
17 And have you not openly admitted this in the full light of day?
18 Are not these spoils laden upon you as upon a burden-donkey?
19 That is my statement: if you are honest with me what can you answer?
20 What profit will you gain by denial? I have clearly established my case.
21 Concerning your plea: 'Do not incite the Ogaadeen against us' I also have a complaint.

* * * * *

22 As to your statement 'We have not seen the sailing ship'[1] I also have a complaint.
23 Why are you tiring yourself out,[2] working your wiles?
24 Do you not get weary with pointless talk?
25 Who rules the sea and controls the sails and holds of ships?
26 The Italians are your followers, the foundlings whom you drive with you;
27 Had they not been led by you they would not have come to Dannood,
28 They would not have sent an expedition to Doollo and ʿIid;

[1] Here the Sayyid refers to his claim that one of his dhows had been intercepted by the British.

[2] Lit. 'Why are you dying, running fast with deceit?'

7 Wachaan Kaa dalbahayaa — duunkaagu wuchuu qabo
8 Intaad dawlad u tahay — adigaa u damiin ah e
9 Ma waa diidi nimankaad — dabatay e i soo dhacay?

10 Wachay iga dudduubeen — may kor u dabaashaan?

11 May dowga Caadood galbeed — uga dareershaan?

12 Dalkaad adigu joogtiyo — Burco machay ka dooneen?

13 Dar Alliyo heshiis iyo — ma daawaad lahaydeen?
14 Mise waa dayoobeen — doqon baa habowdee?
15 Dabadeed na maalkii — sow dacalka ku ma shuban?

16 Sow daabacaagiyo — daftarkaaga ku ma dhigan?

17 Sow duhur dharaareed — dibnahaaga ka ma qiran?

18 Sow sida dameerka raran — dusha Kaa ma fuushanaa?

19 Haddaad daacad ii tahay — dacwiyay e machaad oran?

20 Dafir miyuu wach Kuu tari? — Daliilkii Ku siiyay e

21 Ogaadeen ha ii dirin — dacwad baan ka leeyahay

* * * * *

22 Doonnidii ma arag — dacwad baan ka leeyahay

23 War, machaad durduradiyo — dilacanta ugu diman?
24 Hadal aan dawo lahayn — sow ka ma diiqootaan?
25 Dakhalkiyo shiraaciyo badda — yaa ka dawli yah?
26 Talyanku waa dadkaagiyo — daayiciinka aad wadato

27 Haddii aadan duqlaalayn — Dannood soo ma aadeen?

28 Diraac Doollo iyo Ciid — duullaan ku ma yimaaddeen

29 They would not have sent their armies against me.
30 They would not have harassed me with assaults at daybreak.
31 I had no issue with the Italians until you summoned them to your aid.
32 It was you who intrigued and plotted with them;
33 It was you who said 'Join us in the war against the Dervishes';
34 And they did not say 'Leave us, and stop conspiring with us';
35 Did you never tire of these evil machinations?
36 Was it not through these schemes that the landings at Obbia took place?
37 Did they not greatly aid you with their arms and supplies?
38 You fools, those who attacked yesterday on your side
39 Will they not strike at me from the back if we fight tomorrow?
40 Will they be prevented from attacking me, by disclaiming their bond with you?[1]
41 It is you who lead to pasture these weaker infidels;
42 Can I distinguish between you and your livestock?
43 As to your statement 'We have not seen the sailing ship', I also have a complaint.

* * * * *

44 As to the raiders of whom you talk, I also have a complaint.
45 It is you who have oppressed them and seized their beasts,
46 It is you who took for yourselves their houses and property,
47 It is you who spoilt their settlements and defiled them with ordure,
48 It is you who reduced them to eating the tortoise and beast of prey;
49 This degradation you brought upon them.
50 If they (in turn) become beasts of prey and loot you
51 And steal small things from the clearings between your huts,
52 Then they were driven to this by hunger and famine;
53 Do not complain to me and I will not complain to you.
54 If you do not accept my statement,
55 And unless your servants confuse you with lies,
56 That I harboured them, or that I sent them against you,
57 Bring me clear evidence; otherwise it is you who are guilty of the sin.

[1] Lit. 'Will they become fenced off by (the words) "(You) are not my company (or allies)?"'

Deegaanyo ciidam ah dusha   iga ma keeneen
Dildilow waa beri weerar   igu ma daasheen
Durqun na ma dhech joogin e   adaa hiil ka daalibay

Adigaa duraamiyo   docogeysi ula tegay
Adaa yiri, daraawiish   dagaalkeeda ii raac
Asna diradiraynti   iga deyso ku ma oran
Intaad deli dhacayseen   sow kula ma daalayn?
Sow daraaddii ku ma iman   Hobyo wichii ka soo degay?

Sow dab iyo chooliyo   dabad Kuu ma caawinin?
War, nin shalay, damiinyohow,   igu dilay daraaddaa
Berri haddaynu dirirno na   dusha iga wareentayn?
Daawadayda ma ahayn   ma ku deyrsamayaa?

Durufleyda gaalaad   adaa daaqsanaayee
Ma waan kala duwayaa   adiyo duunkaa?
Doonnidii ma arag   dacwad baan ka leeyahay

* * * * *

Dabatada aad sheegto na   dacwad baan ka leeyahay
War, adaa dulleeyoo   duunyadii ka qaadee
Adaa deeblohoodii   dabaqada ku jiitee
Adaa degelladoodii   digachaar ka mariyee

Diinka iyo dugaaggiyo   adaa duufka siiyay e

Intaas oo darchumo ah   adigaa u diiqay e
Haddii ay dugaagaan oo   wach Kaa durqaamaan
Oo wach aan duch gelinayn   duleeddada ka chadaan

Iyaga ba dan gaajiyo   diihaal baa u geeyay
Adigu na dan hayga gelin   anna haygu digo gelin
Dayib haddaadan oranayn   dabuubtaan ku leeyahay
Oo dochorrayaashii   been Kugu dakhaakhuli
Bal inaan dugsi u ahay   amaan idinku soo diray
Haddii aadan danbaabayn,   daahir marag ah soo taag

58 As to the raiders of whom you talk, I also have a complaint.

* * * * *

59 Concerning your demand 'Turn aside from the Warsangeli', I have a complaint.
60 If they prefer you, then they and I shall be at variance:
61 It is not in my nature to accept people who cringe to you.
62 But if they are Dervishes, how can I turn aside from them?
63 Do you also share their ancestry from Daarood Ismaa'iil?[1]
64 Are you trying to steal towards me through my ancestor's genealogy?
65 Of late have you not turned them into gazelles,[2] (fugitive and homeless)?
66 Have you not seen how they loathe you?
67 For have you not seized their shops and stored their goods in your houses?
68 Have you not set fire to their ships so that smoke rose from them?
69 You, with your filthy genitals, have you not hanged their men?
70 They soon found out that you would have no mercy on them.
71 You are against both worship and the Divine Law.
72 You are building a mat partition between them and the streams of Paradise and Heaven.
73 You are casting them into the raging fury and fumes of Hell.
74 Do they not see how deceitful you are?
75 Or are they well pleased with your prevarication?
76 Will they be divorced from their womenfolk and wives?[3]

* * * * *

[1] Daarood Ismaa'iil, the eponymous ancestor of the Daarood clans to which the Sayyid belongs and which include the Warsangeli. The Sayyid refers to the fact that while the Warsangeli are of one blood with him, the British have no connexion with them, and therefore in Somali values, no claims upon their loyalty.

[2] Lit. 'Did you not turn them into Speke's gazelles (*deero*) and Soemering's gazelles (*'awl*).' In our interpretation gazelles symbolize here living in deserted places, away from human habitations, in constant fear and always on the move. We have also heard of another possible interpretation of this line: the Sayyid apparently refers to the internal split which occurred among the Warsengeli, when those who sided with him would no longer associate with those who opposed him. The two different species of gazelle mentioned in this line live in separate herds.

[3] This passage is very obscure. Literally it means: 'Are they divorcing their womenfolk, they have divorced their wives?' Most probably this amounts to a rhetorical question 'Are they becoming apostates from Islam?' According to oral traditions the Sayyid declared that marriages of those men who refused to follow him became void on the legal grounds of apostasy from Islam. Their wives were therefore automatically divorced and were bound to leave them.

58 Dabatada aad sheegto na   dacwad baan ka leeyahay

* * * * *

59 Warsangeli doc uga bayr   dacwad baan ka leeyahay

60 Mar hadday Ku doortaan   is ku diirad ma ihin
61 Dabigaygu ma oggola   nin Ku dallaasa e
62 Daraawiish hadduu yahay   sidee doc uga leechdaa?
63 War, Daarood Ismaaciil   diir miyaad wadaagtaan?
64 Durriyadii adoogay   miyaanad igu duur chulin?

65 War, sow deero iyo cawl   adiga Kaa ma digin?

66 Inay se Kuu dudahayaan   sow ma ba dareensanid?
67 Sow dukaammadoodii   daarahaaga ku ma guran?

68 Sow doonyohoodii dukhaan   naar ah ku ma shidin?

69 Sow dooraweynow,   ma deldelin raggoodii?
70 Inaanad doclilaynin   diyaar ku ogaade
71 Dikrigii iyo shareecadda   labadaad ka doodi ye
72 Durdurkii Fardoosiyo   Jannadaad ka daahi ye

73 Darbadii Cadaabkiyo   dukhaankii baad ku tuuri ye
74 War, inaad dagaysanayd   sow dareemi maayaan?
75 Ma Ku diirsanayaan   deelqaafkan aa tiri?
76 Dumarkii ma furayaan   chilihi dalaaqe?

* * * * *

77 Concerning your demand 'Return the camels', I have a complaint.[1]
78 I also have suffered damage and loss;
79 You threw me on the ground and skinned my knee,
80 It was you who snatched the camels as they grazed,
81 It was you who scattered the white-turbanned army,
82 It was I who was first hammered at Gallaadi and experienced your bitterness;
83 A fool understands nothing, but the warning did not elude me.
84 The tethering rope with which you bound ʿIise[2] was meant for me,
85 And unless he is released at once there will be no peace in the world.
86 I uttered a cry, asserting my rights, so that I may not be wronged;
87 Do not expect generosity from me: yet shall we make a bargain?
88 And shall we agree to what is in our mutual interest?
89 Or fall upon each other? God knows who is the oppressed.
90 Oh, leave trickery behind and decide today, now!

6. *The Road to Damnation*

MAḤAMMED ʿABDILLE ḤASAN

This poem is a sermon in poetic form in which the Sayyid sets out some of the main principles of Islam and boasts of his orthodox adherence to them. He contrasts his own piety with the infidelity and evil lives of his opponents. The tone of the poem is characteristic of the Sayyid's policy throughout the war which he conducted. He declared that he wanted to restore the purity of Islam among the Somalis and to set up a pastoral theocracy, nationalist and transcending clan loyalties. Whoever opposed him was branded as an enemy of Islam. The effectiveness of this approach brought many adherents into his camp and gained for him sympathizers even amongst the enemy clans.

1 The reference here is to livestock seized from the clans friendly to the British by the Sayyid's forces.

2 ʿIise was the captain of the dhow referred to in line 22 and allegedly captured by the British.

77 Geelii soo dareersha na   dacwad baan ka leeyahay

78 Aniga ba duunkar   dacataa i gaaray e
79 Dibirrootigaagaa   lowgu igu diirmay
80 Qayradii dareernayd adaa   damag ka siiyay e
81 Raggii duubcadda ahaa   adaa deli ka chooray e
82 Dubbihii Gallaadiyo   dudmaa ii horraysay e

83 Damiin baan wach garanin e   digniin ii ma laabnee

84 Dabar Ciise Lagu chiray   anaa Laygu dooni ye

85 Degdeg haddaan Loo furin   dunidaa fasaadin e

86 Dantay baan la yeedhay   yaan Laygu diimin

87 Deeq iga ma juusee   wach ma kala dullaalnaa?

88 Oo wichii dan inoo ah   maysu yeelnaa?
89 Mise ways daboolnaa?   Nin dulmiyan Allaa og e
90 War, ha dagannin maantee   kala dooro maantaas!

Ḥuseen, the person to whom the poem is addressed, was one of Sheikh Maḥammed's constant attendants whose main function was to memorize and later broadcast his poetry.

1 Ḥuseen, I have words for you, listen well:
2 Brother, the faith we received, I hold in high esteem,
3 The sayings of our Lord are the words which I love.
4 At the hours of prayer it is my duty to cleanse myself,
5 Each day of the Ramadan fast I must abstain from food,
6 To withhold even a single kid from the alms of obligation would be to transgress my duty.
7 I must forswear all neglect of my faith,
8 All the obligatory tasks I must fulfil;
9 I must eschew any neglect which has endangered my soul,
10 It is my duty to earn some merit for the day of judgment,
11 It is my duty to kill a ram for the sheikh laden with his books,
12 And in a sheltered spot I should spread my straw mat for him,
13 And he should be regaled with the best meat of the rump and belly.
14 But I should beware the son of Walabe and his like,
15 And if he says 'Give me something', it is my duty to sink my spear in him.
16 Those who come to me with threats, it is my duty to challenge.
17 It is my duty to attack the Hagar[1] lineage, with their cankered testicles;
18 It is my duty to destroy their dwindling herds,
19 And those of them who are impoverished and destitute should be driven to the river,[2]
20 While those who are left behind should be eaten slowly by birds of prey.
21 The fate of the Iidoor peoples[3] is to remain forever as stupid as donkeys;
22 And since the day of Adam, it is their lot to trot in terror behind the infidels,

1 *Hagar*, see *Ḥiin Finiin, the Poet's Favourite Horse*, note 5, p. 68.

2 The reference here is probably to the Shebelle (Shabeelle) River, the more northerly of the two permanently flowing watercourses of the Somali Republic.

3 *Iidoor* is a derogatory name sometimes given to the Isaaq clans by the Daarood.

1 Chuseenow, war baan Kuu hayaa   wachaad tidhaa weeye
2 Walaalow, wacdiga Layna faray   ila wanaag weeye
3 Waanada Astaadkeennu yidhi   weedh aan rabo weeye
4 Weysada salaadeed inaan   waachidsado weeye
5 Wannahaarka soon inaanan soor   waa na cunin weeye
6 Wachadayda maal inaanan dago   wachar ku deyn weeye

7 Diintaan wadeecada ka dhigay   inaan walayn weeye
8 Wichii waajiboo idil inaan   wada gutaa weeye
9 Wahsi baa naftii iga jaree   inaan wirfaa weeye
10 Walbahaarka Aakhiro inaan   wuch u tabcaa weeye
11 Wadaadkii kitaabbo leh inaan   wan u qalaa weeye

12 Weylaalis inaan meel dugsoon   ugu wadhaa weeye

13 Walanqihiyo dhayada inuu   walafsadaa weeye

14 Ina Walaban oo kale inaan   weger idhaa weeye
15 Wach i sii hadduu yadhi inaan   waran daraa weeye

16 Walasaqo wichii iila yami   inaan wirayn weeye

17 Winifiirle Reer Hagar inaan   weerar gelin weeye

18 Wayaakada adduunka ah inaan   wiririf siin weeye
19 Wirriskooda caydheed inuu   webi tagaa weeye

20 Wayaaggii ka soo hadhay inuu   haad waywayo weeye

21 Iidoorku weligiis inuu   wadal ahaa weeye

22 Woqood Aadankood inay kufriga   dabo washlayn weeye

23 They are fated to understand nothing and condemned to madness,
24 Their lot is to hate the faith and to despise the Divine Law;
25 Let them bring upon themselves a curse, these children of the devil,
26 It is their fate to bring sorrow to those who turn with zeal to the holy war,
27 Outcast sorcerers[1] are destined never to breathe the sweet airs of heaven,
28 Their lot is to limp feebly along the road to Hell,
29 My portion is to walk in the company of the Sura of Watiin[2] and the blessing of Divine Praise.

7. *The Path of Righteousness*

MAḤAMMED ʿABDILLE ḤASAN

In this poem the Sayyid exhorts his listeners to obey conscientiously the injunctions of Islam, urging that anyone who is a good Muslim must follow him and eschew compromise with the infidels, the Sayyid's enemies in the holy war.

The contrast between virtue and vice, fidelity and apostasy, wisdom and foolishness, bravery and cowardice, generosity and meanness, are the recurring themes of the poem. Throughout Sheikh Maḥammed makes it clear that it is profitable and fitting to be in friendship and fellowship with a pious and righteous man like himself, while to associate with the vile enemies of Islam leads only to disappointment and disaster. The poem is typical of his technique of dealing with people. The poet alternates between gentle exhortation and violent condemnation as he seeks to overcome all opposition and reduce his enemies to confusion.

1 He who knows God and follows the Divine Law
2 He who does not forget the profession of faith which was set before him
3 And who does not deny it; the truth must be upheld!
4 He who regularly observes the obligatory prayers at their times

[1] 'Outcast sorcerers', lit. 'the Yibirs'. The Yibir are a small, widely scattered people who live mainly as itinerant pedlars and soothsayers amongst the Somali. By Somali they are traditionally regarded as outcasts, and generally feared as sorcerers. In physical features and general cultural characteristics, however, they closely resemble the Somali.

[2] The ninety-fifth Sura of the Quran, called 'The Fig'.

23 Wachba inaanu garanaynin oo   waalanyahay weeye

24 Wachyigiyo Shareecada inay   wada naceen weeye
25 Waleecaad ha fuulee iblays   werisadiis weeye

26 Nin jahaad u weyrachay inay   wahan geeyaan weeye

27 Walwalkii Jannada inaan Yibruhu   waa na urin weeye

28 Waddada naarta Loo maro inay   walagsadaan weeye
29 Anna inaan Watiin iyo chamdiga   weheshadaa weeye

1 Nin Ilaah yaqaan oo Sharciga   ku isticmaalaaya
2 Ashahaado Loo qoray nin aan   kala illaaweynin

3 Oo aan inkirahayn; chaq waa   La oggolaadaa ye
4 Nin salaadda awqaadda faral   u addimoonaaya

5 And he who fulfils the duties of charity and seeks what is perfect
6 And who does not break the ıast; the month of Ramadan is holy.
7 And he who gives of his property and livestock with sincerity
8 And who makes no parade of his gifts
9 And whose ancestors were never accused of meanness.[1]
10 He who does not fall into heresy in the last stages of time[2]
11 And who does not follow the Amharas as though they were his fathers
12 And who does not fight as an askari for the uncircumcised infidel
13 And who does not turn up his nose at the origins and ways of the Somali
14 And who does not perform menial services for the wages of the unbelievers
15 Or accept without complaint their niggardly wage;
16 He who devotes himself to the holy war and is garlanded with flowers
17 He who turns against the English dogs
18 And who wins the victory and glory and the shouts and songs of praise.
19 Oh see how stupidity leads to disappointment!

20 Quarrels are not good, truth is where one should water.
21 Is not he who is known for all these good things a true Muslim?

* * * * *

22 The meeting summoned,[3] the elders' speeches done, the matter in dispute,
23 The gates slammed shut, the doors closed, and the problem unsolved,
24 When resort is had to a clever man, to a sheikh, and to elders
25 And the dispute is so intertwined that no settlement can be found

[1] This line must not be interpreted literally. The poet refers to mean people in general.

[2] The last stages of time, i.e. the time preceding the end of the world, when, it is believed, much confusion will arise.

[3] This line and the five lines which follow it refer to the ability of a person to bring peace and to settle disputes, a quality which is considered one of the greatest accomplishments of a clever and righteous man.

5 Oo dagada oofinahayoo   ugubka soocaaya

6 Oo aan afurin, Soonku waa   bilaha iideed e

7 Adduunyadiyo choolaha ninkii   aragti dhiibaaya
8 Oo inuu ahooyey yiraa   ka istichoonaya
9 Oo aan bakhaylnimo abkii   Lagu inshaaraynin
10 Nin aan diinta aafadi geleyn   aakhiruu sebenka
11 Oo aan Amchaarada sidii   aabo u yaacaynin

12 Aan gaalka ooradu ku taal   u askarahaynin

13 Aan abuurka Soomaaliyeed   ka anfitaageynin

14 Oo aan ajuurada kufriga   ugu adeegeynin

15 Oo aan ardiga beesadeed   u ashtakooneynin
16 Nin jahaad ahoominahayoo   ubacha Loo saaray

17 Ingriiska eyga ah ninkii   ugu leechaaya
18 Oo libin ajri leh soo heloo   or iyo geeraar leh

19 Nimanyohow, oqoonchumadu waa   eeragoysnimo e
20 Asaraar ma fiicna e run baa   Lagu arooraa ye
21 Ninkii aynigaas Lagu yaqaan   sow Islaam ma aha?

* * * * *

22 Shir aguugay, waayeel abyamay   talo asheedowday

23 Irdo jiq ah, albaabbo is ku chiran   eel La bichin waayay

24 Nin oqoon leh aw iyo haddii   odayo Loo geeyo
25 Chaajada afraha duubatee   Loo olmami waayay

26 Although day after day the efforts to reach a conclusion continue
27 Is not he a wise man who finally succeeds in bringing agreement?

* * * * *

28 When the cries for help rise up
29 And when arms are taken to the fields of battle
30 And when the bay horse wades through the sand and dust
31 On that day when men break their spears in chest and spine
32 When the vulture falls upon the spewed out meat
33 And when the din of battle resounds all around
34 When the coward drops his weapons and abandons you for flight
35 When those who are out of sight of others steal away like game
36 On that day is not he who fights bravely like a lion attacking?

* * * * *

37 He who is not wicked; shameful deeds are polluting

38 He who does not inveigh against you without foundation
39 And who shows respect and restraint towards you
40 He who spreads goodness evenly among all the sons of Adam
41 He who does not favour those to whom he is close in genealogical descent
42 He who does not sow dissension amongst the slaves of God
43 He who holds his peace and is silent when evil words are spoken to him
44 He who does not bring trouble to those with whom he stays
45 And who does not cut open again the stomach of an inflammatory issue
46 He who does not tremble with excitement at the prospect of profit and food
47 And who does not eat to the last morsel the dish placed before him
48 And who does not gorge himself like a glutton gobbling food
49 He who does not threaten others with violence, endangering his own house
50 He who does not conceal his pot of buttermilk
51 And he who does not secrete his skin bag of ghee in the innermost part of his house

26 In kastoo ayaan iyo ayaan   amarka Loo guulo

27 Ninkii maalintaa ka arrinshaa   aaqil sow ma aha?

* * * * *

28 Uu'uu'da qaylada haddii   uubatadu yeedhdho
29 Sengootida ilwaadda leh haddii   agabta Loo qaato
30 Awaaraha buska leh maalintuu   chamar abraaraayo
31 Maalintii warmaha oofta iyo   arachda Lays gooyo
32 Maantuu aboodigu ku lali   amacha Loo daadshay
33 Maantuu asaayuhu ka dhici   idil dagaalkeeda
34 Maantuu fuluhu Kaa ordo ee   alabas rooraayo

35 Maantuu raggaan Loo ilayn   wada ugaaroobo

36 Maantaas ninkii aarsan sow   aarka dhici ma aha?

* * * * *

37 Nin aan edebdarroonayn chil waa   Laga ajoodaa ye
38 Aflagaaddo aan jirin nin aan   Kuula imanaynin
39 Oo Kaa asluubsanyahay oo   Ku istichaynaaya
40 Ab uu yahay ba aadmiga ninkii   samo ekaynaaya
41 Abtirsiimo kii chigay nin aan   iniq u dheeraynin

42 Addoomaha Ilaahay nin aan   kala irdhaynaynin
43 Ninkii aammusoo shib ah haddii   eray chun Loo diiqo

44 Aan kula akeekamin intaa   ururka uu joogo
45 Aan chaajo awgeed La gubay   ubucda jeechaynin

46 Anfaacigiyo dhuuniga nin aan   ku anfariiraynin

47 Aan cheero soor Lagu akhtimay   eber ka yeelaynin

48 Oo sida ardaallada wach cuni   alam ka siinaynin
49 Intuu aqalka baanjiyo ninkaan   aradka guulguulin

50 Aagaanta ciirta ah ninkaan   aaska dhiganaynin
51 Oo aan qumbaha awdan oo   ilachirkaw jiidan

52 He who received a favour and who recognized it
53 And who will do you a favour as long as the world retains its scent
54 And he who does not know ingratitude, is he not worthy of respect?

* * * * *

55 Many sheep and goats, cattle, camels, all the riches of the world
56 Stock bearing for the first time, she-camels, not fully-grown, that have calved and whose young have been killed,
57 A herd of fine horses, and horses which speed across the land,
58 A big house, a bridal chamber for which mats of brilliant hue were made,
59 A girl as beautiful as a necklace or costly clothes,
60 Wearing a necklace of heavy beads which murmur (as she walks);
61 He who brought you sincere counsel, prosperity, and livestock,
62 He who answers all your needs,
63 Who in this world and the next works for your profit
64 Who welcomes you like a kinsman in your day of need
65 And who at the height of the drought does not bar his gate against you,
66 Is not he who never fails you in your weakness one of the brethren?

8. *A Message to the Ogaadeen*

MAḤAMMED ʿABDILLE ḤASAN

This poem was addressed by the Sayyid to the Ogaadeen clan, exhorting them to abandon any alliances with the British and Ethiopians and to join him. There are several references to individual lineages of the Ogaadeen whose lack of support the poet deplores.

1 Oh Ḥasan,[1] you have collected together your weapons, and now as you leave us
2 My heart rejoices at the decision you have come to.

[1] Ḥasan, who is also referred to as Ḥuseen in line 40, is the emissary.

52 Aaqibo Loo galay nin ay   aakid u ahaatay
53 Oo Kuu ichsaan fali intuu   udug adduun joogo

54 Oo aan abaaldhaca oqoon   sow ikhyaar ma aha?

* * * * *

55 Ari badan, lo' iyo geel intii   mulug adduunyaad ah

56 Ugub dhalaya, qaalmo ummuloo   Laga unuun gooyay

57 Eeraan fardood iyo gammaan   aradka duulaaya
58 Aqal weyn, aroos ilicyiyo   ilachir Loo yeelay

59 Inan quruchsan oo Lagu ashbahay   awsi iyo khayli
60 Oo qool asli yah Loo geshoo   jalamtu eedaamin

61 Naasich iyo wanaag iyo ninkii   ilindi Kuu keenay

62 Umuurtii aad leedahay ninkii   Kuu ebyoonahaya
63 Adduunka iyo aakhiro ninkii   Kuu aslaachahaya
64 Ninkii maalintaad iillantahay   aano Kugu qaatay
65 Oo aan abaaraha dhag yiri   oodda Kugu jiidin

66 Itaalchumo na Kaagaga tegayn   sow ikhwaan ma aha?

1 Chasanow! Hub qaadday e had-daad   naga hagaagayso
2 Hiyigaad ka sara joogsatay   hibatay laabtii ye

3 When in the early morning, at dawn, you rise and mount your stallion,
4 Apart from the sand and dust that rises up around you, the columns of dust,
5 The road which you will follow is not one on which people lose their way
6 And indeed it is straight from here to Hiiraan.
7 Nevertheless, what the Haud is known for is hardship and lack of water.
8 The present season is the time of the light Kaliil[1] rains.
9 God who fills our water-ponds will not make you thirst.
10 Bush thick and impenetrable, scorched *ḥagar*[2] trees, the hot air rising from them,
11 Hot wind and heat, which will lick you like a flame,
12 A mantle of air and a shade-giving tree will shelter you;
13 The swelling of feet pricked by thorns, a thorny thicket, plants prickly and spiny,
14 Charred plants, hot stumps of burned trees, the hot air rising from them,
15 The burnt branches and tree trunks through which you will pass will not harm you.
16 A bull-rhinoceros, ready to jump, a male lion, angry and roaring in attack,
17 The goring with the head, the clutching of claws, the biting fang,
18 The giraffe's rocking gait, the kicking of the leg, the elephant flying,
19 The hyena's attack, the beasts of prey, open-mouthed, panting for meat,
20 A leopard attacking in daylight, the fox sneaking away, a cheetah growling,
21 A hairy hyena, a maned hyena skulking in hidden places, a pack of wolves,
22 Creeping beasts, evil reptiles, venomous, bearing poison;
23 The robbers who roam, the raiders, the fugitives, the thieves;
24 The small bustard with its piteous cry, the great bustard whose heart trembles;

[1] Light rains falling before the main spring wet season.
[2] A species of *Commiphora*.

3	Haddaad hiirta waa beri sengaha	halabsatoo fuushid
4	Habaas idinku duula iyo boor	hirif ah mooyaane
5	Hilinkaad ku dhici waa mid aan	laga habaabayn e
6	Waa tuu haloosiga ahaa	tan iyo Hiiraan e
7	Ha yeesho e wach Hawd Lagu ya-qaan	hawkar iyo oon e
8	Hadda aynu joognaa na waa	hogo kaliileed e
9	Allihii harada noo buuchin jiray	ku ma haraadsiiyo
10	Hinni oodan chagar huuraa	oo halaw ka soo duulo
11	Hanfiga iyo kulaykoo sidii	halac Ku leefaaya
12	Hagoog layr ah harac Kaa astura	LaGugu hoosaas ye
13	Hurgun gocondho hiil qodach leh	iyo hiiji iyo qaarri
14	Hurmood gubad leh dogob huuro leh	oo halaw ka soo duulo
15	Hirrigtaad maraysiyo jirduhu	Ku ma halaakeeyo
16	Wiyil hadaf ah, aar soo handaday	hiijo qaba reemi
17	Hardi madach hantoobsiga cidida	mici haleelaysa
18	Hurdub geri, harraatida lugeed	qalamje heeraaya
19	Hullufaac dhurwaa iyo dugaag	so' u hadaaqaaya
20	Shabeel horor ah, haaribo dawoco	haramcad guuchaaya
21	Dhidar halab leh halowyaalo weer	haalifada yey ah
22	Bahal hoose halaq baas intii	had iyo waabay leh
23	Haaweyda meertiyo colkiyo	haaribkiyo tuugga
24	Galow hiririfleeyiyo jugley	wadane hawhawleh

25 The heat of the rainless season, the desolate terrain, losing the way;
26 I invoke the saints who keep the straight path, and the riches of the Sura of Yaasiin,[1]
27 May God, day and night, turn danger away from you,
28 Before you, on each side and behind, everywhere, may the peace of God be upon you;
29 May your home be surrounded by the blessing of Watiin,[2] may your night sojourn enjoy the blessing of the Sura of Liilaaf,[3]
30 I have bestowed much blessing upon you: say amen to the gift!
31 Say: These four blessings are like the sound of heavy rain
32 And like a small shower from a rain-holding cloud, drop by drop I let my words fall upon you;
33 A torrent has not issued from me.
34 Although I am in great anger I have tempered my words, fearing for you.
35 If I became like thunder, you would drown in the waves of my wrath
36 And in the noise the lightning would blind you;
37 The air would be great black waves round you.
38 You would fly for your life from the blast that came forth from me.
39 You will not find the equal to this poem I am reciting.
40 On account of Ḥuseen I have died from hunger and thirst
41 But he has failed to understand the wisdom which I have placed before him.
42 Take a few words from me to your clan, when you reach Hagidi:
43 Tell everyone that it is shameful to shirk duty.
44 Proclaim the message to the women, to the children, and to grown men.
45 Ibraahiim,[4] whose clan I am, gives me no support.
46 They are near kinsmen, of the same flesh and blood and maternal ancestor.

[1] The sixty-sixth Sura of the Quran, generally considered as the heart of the sacred book.

[2] The ninety-fifth Sura of the Quran, called 'The Fig'.

[3] The hundred and sixth Sura of the Quran, called 'The Quraysh'.

[4] A lineage of the Ogaadeen.

25 Habheebaha jidaashiyo dalkiyo hanaq go'i dawga

26 Weliyada hanuunaan beryiyo hodonka Yaasiin e

27 Habeen iyo dharaar Eebbahay hadimo Kaa baaji
28 Hor iyo gees hareer iyo gadaal halal nabaddiino

29 Hoygaagu heeraar Waatiin hoyasho Liilaaf leh

30 Hayaakiil ducaan Kuu naqay e hibada Aammiin dheh

31 Afartaa sidii heego roob hababacdeedii dheh
32 Sida hogol daruur curatay baan hibitiqaayaa ye

33 Harawaatigii iga ma iman hoorista ahaa ye
34 Wachaasaan habuurayn adaan Kuu hawilayaa ye

35 Haddaan Kugu hanqaro mawjad-daad ku harfan doontaa ye
36 Hillaacaa indhaha Kaala tegi halalacdiisii ye
37 Hawadaa wachay Kula ahaan hirar madow weyn e
38 Hinnifka iga soo bachay naftaad kala harbaysaa ye

39 Heli maysid gabaygaan hayiyo hiiyi waalaha e
40 Chuseen baan hagoog ugu dhintiyo haq iyo looyaan e
41 Isagu ba higgaaddaan u dhigay heli oqoon waa ye

42 Hal yar iiga gee Reer Tolkaa Hagidi aad gaarto

43 Hebelkii walbeetaba u sheeg hagari waa ceeb e
44 Haweenka iyo carruurta iyo nin weyn harawaduu naadi
45 Ibraahiimku haybtaan ahaa wuusan hadi hayn e
46 Waa wada qaraabiyo hilbiyo habarwadaaggay e

47 A djinn set them against me, otherwise they would not perhaps have harmed me.
48 They did not repay me for the respect and the kindness which I had shown them.
49 They would not have borne false witness against me, or flung grievous abuse at me;
50 The girls when they dance would not have made songs against me;
51 They would not have rejected my preaching, insulting and flaying the Prophet;
52 They would not have supported the infidels with whom we are fighting;
53 They would not have slipped down into the abyss of Hell from Paradise;
54 They would not have gathered against me the hordes with which we are at enmity;
55 When I defeated the infidels they would not have sheltered them;
56 And the Harti,[1] having gone into hiding, would not have fired at me;
57 They would not have married the stupid women of the Habar Magaadle[2] clans.
58 With evil mouths they would not have babbled against me, consenting to evil talk.
59 They would not have pitched their tents in Harar, after taking them from Haro;
60 They would not have been willing to drive the camels so hard that the burden saddles galled them;
61 They would not have fetched firewood for the Indians[3] who live in Berbera;
62 They would not have made their backs sore with carrying loads;
63 They would not have sought relief from hunger from those who earned only a few pence;

[1] A group of clans of the Daarood clan family. It is also possible, however, that the word *Harti* is not the name of the group of clans here, but an archaic noun whose meaning is no longer remembered. Someone suggested to us that it may denote a type of rifle, but we have not been able to find confirmation for this.

[2] One of the main divisions of the Isaaq clans.

[3] Probably a reference to Indian troops stationed at Berbera.

47	Jinnaa igu hudbeeyay e malaha	i ma halaajeen e
48	Hannaankiyo wanaaggaan u galay	haako oran waa ye
49	Hafriin been ah cay igu hab daran	igu ma hoorsheen e
50	Goortay habluhu boodayaan	igu ma heeseen e
51	Hiddaayada ma diideen intay	Nebiga hiifaan e
52	U ma hiiliyeen gaaladaan	heeriga ahayn e
53	Haawiyada Naareed Jannada	uga ma hoobteen e
54	Ii ma soo humeen guutadaan	haayirka ahayn e
55	Goortaan hambooriyay kufriga	igu ma hiileen e
56	Harti igu ma toogteen intuu	hiisha ii galay e
57	Hingaar naago ka ma guursadeen	Habar Magaadlaay e
58	Intay heeh yiraahdaan af baas	ku ma hadaaqeen e
59	Harar ku ma fureen reer intay	Haro ka gooyaan e
60	Hiyi u ma yiraahdeen ratiga	heensihii gubay e
61	Hindigii Berbera joogi jiray	hil u ma qaadeen e
62	Heeryada chammaalka ah garbaha	ma ayan hoosheen e
63	Ninkii halalad beeso ah tabcaday	ma hungureeyeen e

64 They would not have had to fawn upon those young men with whom Hell is overflowing;
65 The people of the world would not have abused them
66 They would not have been driven hither and thither like game on the run
67 The Hayaag,[1] Hulqe, and Khaalid lineages would not have sought to loot them.
68 A vain thought, which could not be, deceived the Makaahiil.[2]
69 They fell into a pit when they abandoned the Darawish
70 They would not have been destroyed had they not entered the Europeans' territory.
71 From the time of Abel we have enjoyed the riches of the Faith;
72 God does not refuse my prayers for grace
73 When I curse a person God cuts his tendon.
74 It was deceit and death that threw you into a deep pit
75 Through mere hardness and obstinacy people perish.
76 Make certain! You are mistakenly rejecting good advice.
77 I wept. I did not like some of the words
78 I shed tears when I received news of them.
79 They (my enemies) cut off the testicles of the party in which Faaqid[3] was.
80 The Haaruun[4] would not have shot those for whom I had great expectations.
81 Hyenas indeed devoured their brave men.
82 The enemy is deceiving you by weeping;
83 While he is giving you advice he is digging your grave
84 While he is advising you he is considering his own interests
85 While they want your respect, they do not intend to respect you.
86 But I can guarantee to give you whatever you want.
87 A thousand that run, thousands of those that are swift and raise their tails,
88 A thousand that raise their necks and vie with the birds of prey,
89 Thousands of saddled ones and thousands without saddles, which are being exercised in Hadi,

[1] Three lineages of the Ḍulbahante clan.
[2] A section of the Ogaadeen clan.
[3] An Ogaadeen sympathizer of the Dervishes.
[4] A section of the Ogaadeen.

64 Ma hadaadumeen wiilashii   Heel ka buuchsamay e

65 Halqigii arlada joogi jiray   ma hargawaacheen e
66 Sidii halal ugaar oo fakaday   La ma horeeyeen e

67 Hayaag iyo Hulqiyo Khaalidyadu   ma hungureeyeen e

68 Hindise aan jirin waa wichii   hoday Makaahiil e
69 Hog wuchuu ku dhacay kolkuu   huray daraawiish e
70 Hadii ayan haad Faranji gelin   La ma halaajeen e

71 Hanti baan Diinta u lahayn   tan iyo Haabiil e
72 Hoodada karaamada Allaan   igu hungaynayn e
73 Goortaan habaaraa Ilaah   heeray boqontii ye
74 Hoobaaq wachaa idinku riday   had iyo looyaan e
75 Hagag iyo qalayf miiran waa   Lagu habaabaa ye
76 Hubsadooy! Tashiga khayrka   waad ka hanfariirtaan e
77 Hilaabooyayeey! Ma aan jeclayn   hadalka qaarkiis e
78 Hoor baa i soo dhacay kolkaan   helay khabaarkood e
79 Horintii lahayd Faaqid bay   haniyo gooyeen e

80 Haaruun ma toogteen kuwaan   ugu han weynaa ye

81 Waa taa waraabuhu harqaday   hanadyadoodii ye
82 Cadaawuhu hilaaboyga waa   idin hodaayaa ye
83 Isagoo hog Kuu qodahayuu   Kuu halaahali ye
84 Halyuu ula dan leeyahay   markuu Kuu halaahali ye
85 In ay haybad Kula doonayaan   Ku ma hawaystaan e

86 Anigaa idiin huba wachaad   ku hanbalyootaan e
87 Kun haloosi kuman hayraf ah   oo dabada hoogaamin

88 Kun halqooqa wada taagay oo   haadda la ciyaara
89 Kuman heeggan kuman haawiya   oo Hadi ku dooyeeya

90 Thousands and thousands of those that glide in the sky when they jump at full gallop.
91 For you I shall put saddles on long-rumped bay horses
92 For you I shall pour many camels into the empty and desolate corrals.
93 You will drink your fill of the milk of milch-camels that have given birth
94 You will fall upon the vessels of sour milk as camels fall upon water.
95 A man with courage has expectations, a fool is idle in his stagnation.
96 One abandons a place where there is loss,
97 One struggles for a place in which there is profit.
98 Weapons, possessions, property, livestock, and gifts without end,
99 Whatever you expect from me, you will receive.
100 Come to me! You will be drenched in God's munificence.

9. *An Elder's Reproof to his Wife*

ʿABDILLAAHI MUUSE

The following verses by a contemporary poet of the older generation express the poet's experience of an unhappy marriage. The wife was very beautiful and of a strong and well-respected lineage, but apparently the poet found her disobedient and lacking in respect for him. His unfortunate match was not made any easier to bear since he claimed to have expended great wealth in marrying but received no substantial dowry.

1 A stream flowing steadily over a stone does not wet its core,

2 But on fertile soil water brings forth fresh grass,
3 Termite mounds when spoken to give no response,
4 A fool's mind is like a house barred,
5 When one tells people something, they profit by it,
6 But you, may God change you, are made worse by advice.
7 There is some remedy for the fools who listen to you,
8 But there is no medicine for a bad wife who refuses good advice;
9 And I was born with nobility of mind and am not readily disturbed by trifles.

90 Kumanyaal hanqaaraha kabtiga   samada heehaabin

91 Heensaan idiin saarayaa   chamarro heeg dheer e
92 Horweynaan ku soo shubin cheeryaha   haawadoo maran e
93 Caanaha haleelada dhashaad   habacsan doontaan e

94 Haamaha karuur aad sidii   heeladuu dhici ye

95 Nin rag aa hamiya caalle waa   hogoshadiisii ye

96 Haydaarto meeshii leh waa   Laga huleelaa ye
97 Waa Lagu hirtaa meel haddii   halabo Kuu taal e
98 Hub iyo maal iyo hanti iyo choolo iyo   hoo aan dam ahaynin
99 Wachaad iga hawaysaan ba   waad iga helaysaan e
100 Soo halalawdaay! Deeqa Allaad   ku harfan doontaan e!

1 Durdurku ba hadduu dhagach dul maro   dihanka qoyn waa ye
2 Meeshii dalaaday biyuhu   doog ka bichiyaan e
3 Dundumooyinkoo Lala hadlaa   damac ma yeeshaan e
4 Ruuchii damiin ii qalbiga   waa ka daar chidhan e
5 Dadku haddii wach Loo sheego ways   derejo dhaamaa ye
6 Alla doori-yeey, hadalku waa   Kaaga darayaa ye
7 Doqontii Ku yeeshaa wuch uun   Lagu dabiibaa ye
8 Dawo ma laha naag chumi hadday   diiddo waanada e

9 Anuun baan nin door ah u dhashay aan   duni ba aafayn e

10 My dissatisfaction goes back even to the times that I visited you after our engagement.[1]
11 Sometimes a fully laden vessel founders with great loss of property,
12 And certainly I received no return at all for the rifles and camels I gave (as bridewealth),
13 Again and again you wearied me, when the word 'obey' brought no response.
14 Neglect, beating, or divorce
15 On one of these three I am resolved: make your choice!

10. *The Rewards of Success*

ISMAAʿIIL MIRE

This poem by Ismaaʿiil Mire, one of the Sayyid's military commanders, and the leader of the Dervish forces at the battle of Dul Madoba, was composed shortly after the collapse of the holy war in 1921. These verses were addressed, pointedly in the final stanza, to the leader of a party of Somali police engaged in restoring order amongst the Ḍulbahante as the Administration began to recover its hold on the population. The Somali policeman in question was, according to the poet, abusing his position to amass wealth at the expense of the public. Such misuse of power leads to disaster as surely as pride always goes before a fall. This is the theme of the poem: it is illustrated by a series of cautionary examples, the characters in which are explained in the notes.

1 The Lord divides the bread amongst all his slaves
2 Taking care of the fishes in the sea and even of the contents of a cup.
3 Everyone will receive what has been prescribed for him;
4 Even though he runs fast or sets out early in the morning or climbs a high hill
5 No one will gain more than his allotted portion: let that be remembered!

* * * * *

[1] 'Visited you after our engagement'; this is conveyed by the term *dadabgal*, a compound word (*dadab* 'a screen', and *gal* 'enter') referring to visits which a man is entitled to pay to his betrothed at her home. The girl entertains her fiancé in a screened shelter and the couple may sometimes spend the night there. But until the marriage is concluded sexual relations are forbidden.

10 Dar Ilaahag wachaan Kaa nebcaa   dadabgalkaagii ye

11 Rag bay se doonni buuchdaa badaa   kaga degaysaa ye

12 Dabkayga iyo geelii ayaan   duri na Lay siin e

13 Kugu daalay dhaacha e haddaan   didibso Kaa waayay

14 Darbo iyo dilliin iyo inaan   diris ba Kaa yeelo
15 Saddechdaa mid baan Kula damcee   adigu soo dooro!

1 Kulligood addoomaha Rabbaw   qaybshay kibistii ye
2 Bad kalluun ku jira kay ku tahay   ama fijaan kooban

3 Nin waliba wichii Loo katibay   waa La kulansiin e
4 In kastuu kabtiyo ama kallaho   ama kur dheer fuulo

5 Nin na inaanu soo korodhsanayn   kaa ha La ogaado!

* * * * *

6 Af Ḥakame[1] reaped the reward of the trouble and hatred
which he stirred up,
7 He said, 'Let 'Ali be cast down,' as he married Kaaha, 'Ali's
bethrothed.
8 'Ali fashioned a great spear and brewed poison for its tip:
9 Oh men, pride brings disaster: let that be remembered.

* * * * *

10 Ina Ammaan's[2] worldly pride won him a whole land,
11 But he was without fear and did not expect to be killed
by the man who assassinated him.
12 Oh men, pride brings disaster; let that be remembered.

* * * * *

13 When 'Artan[3] hung his saddle on the tamarisk tree,
14 The Garaad Faaraḥ lineage were as soft to him as milk
sweet and sour,
15 But when battle was joined at last they became to him as
bitter as poison.
16 Oh men, pride brings disaster: let that be remembered!

* * * * *

17 It was to his overweening worldly pride that Corfield[4] owed
his death;
18 It did not occur to him that young lads could kill him with
their rifles.

[1] Lines 6–9 refer to a long-standing quarrel between two men, Af Ḥakame and 'Ali Duullane, in the course of which the first seized 'Ali's bride as she was on her way to marry him. This led to a series of fierce battles which ended with the death of both men.

[2] Lines 10–12 refer to a successful career of conquest, abruptly terminated when the leader, Ina Ammaan, was murdered by someone against whom no precautions had been taken and from whom aggression was not expected.

[3] Lines 13–16 summarize the fortunes of 'Artan, a great warrior of a lineage of the Ḍulbahante clan. Such was his reputation for bravery that the mere sight of his saddle perched on the branches of a tree was sufficient to keep the enemy at bay. Yet at last the Garaad Faaraḥ, his enemies, plucked up courage and engaged 'Artan and his kin in battle. 'Artan lost his life.

[4] Lines 17–18 recall the death of Richard Corfield at the battle of Dul Madoba between the British and Dervish forces in 1913. Isma'aiil Mire is well qualified to speak of this incident since he led the Dervish attack. Corfield's death, with other heavy casualties on the British side, was attributed to his supreme self-confidence and rash action in engaging the enemy without adequate numbers or resources and in underestimating the power of the Sayyid's forces. The literal translation of line 17 is: 'To (the words) "It is I alone who own the world" Corfield attributed blame (for his death).'

6 Af Chakame karkabaddii u ay   iyo kulaylkii ye

7 Ka dambee Caluu yidhi intuu   Kaaha guursaday e

8 Kii kale na kaal weyn u tumay   kari na waabay e
9 Ragow, kibirka waa Lagu kufaa   kaa ha La ogaado!

* * * * *

10 Keysaa adduun Ina Ammaan   koos dhan buu helay e
11 Kolla kii arsaa'ilay ma hadin   ka ma na yaabayn e

12 Ragow, kibirka waa Lagu kufaa   kaa ha La ogaado!

* * * * *

13 Cartan dhuurta kooraa markuu   kor ugu laalaayay
14 Garaad Faarach dhay iyo karuur   kala macaanaa ye

15 Misna kala chadhaadhaa dhunkaal   kulankii goobeed e

16 Ragow, kibirka waa Lagu kufaa   kaa ha La ogaado!

* * * * *

17 Anaa dunida keligay leh buu   Koofil eersaday e

18 Kashiisa na ma gelin wiilal baa   keebka Kuu quban e

19 Oh men, pride brings disaster: let that be remembered!

* * * * *

20 He who drinks joyfully from the cup of prosperity and owns a herd of milch-camels
21 Will surely lose his good fortune as it is written.
22 The whole Hagar[1] people were brought to ruin by the claim 'I am the king';
23 Oh men, pride brings disaster; let that be remembered!

* * * * *

24 Long ago Sugulle[2] made a childish mistake,
25 It was poor reasoning that drove him to it, for he and the woman were only distantly connected.
26 Oh men, pride brings disaster: let that be remembered!

* * * * *

27 Ina Galayḍ[3] repented of his words in the end;
28 There would have been no trouble had he brought the she-camel,
29 He whom Ina Galayḍ despised would not then have pierced his kidneys with a spear.
30 Oh men, pride brings disaster; let that be remembered!

* * * * *

31 The six groups of 'Ali Geri[4] who almost destroyed each other
32 Failed to understand the words: 'This is a watering trough and we can mend it ourselves.'
33 Oh men, pride brings disaster; let that be remembered!

* * * * *

[1] This line refers to a series of defeats suffered by the Hagar lineage of the Ḍulbahante clan after a period of great prosperity which had led them to be proud and boastful.

[2] Sugulle interfered without invitation and without authority in a dispute involving a woman to whom he was only distantly related. His unwelcome participation provoked a feud in which he and his kinsmen were heavily defeated.

[3] This man, an elder, had twelve grown-up sons while he was still quite young. One of his sons killed a man of another group and when Ina Galayḍ's lineage were collecting the hundred camels due in compensation for death, Ina Galayḍ himself refused to make any contribution. In these circumstances the offended group refused to accept the incomplete damages and attacked their adversaries. Ina Galayḍ's section was defeated and he himself was captured and executed.

[4] Here the reference is to fierce internecine strife which broke out amongst all the six segments of the 'Ali Geri lineage of the Ḍulbahante clan following a trivial quarrel over precedence in watering at a well. The quarrel started when one man drove his spear through the watering trough of another as he was waiting to water his stock.

Ragow, kibirka waa Lagu kufaa   kaa ha La ogaado!

* * * * *

Ninkii koob nimco ah fuuqsada   e kadin irmaan yeeshaa

In karuurka uu qubo horay   kaafka ugu tiil e
Kulligiis wachaa rogay anaa   kiin ah Reer Hagar e

Ragow, kibirka waa Lagu kufaa   kaa ha La ogaado!

* * * * *

Kamma' Sugulle waagii sidii   kuray carruureed e
Kaschumaa wadday e naagta way   kala fogaayeen e

Ragow, kibirka waa Lagu kufaa   kaa ha La ogaado!

* * * * *

Kalaankuu lahaa Ina Galaydh   kahey gadaalkii ye
Kaarku ba ma joogeen hadduu   keeno tuluddii ye

Baallacad kelyaa ku ma jareen   kii uu quudhsaday e

Ragow, kibirka waa Lagu kufaa   kaa ha La ogaado!

* * * * *

Lichda koos e Reer Cali Geri   e kaw is kaga siiyay
Kasi waaye wuchu waa qabaal   waa na kabannaa ye

Ragow, kibirka waa Lagu kufaa   kaa ha La ogaado!

* * * * *

34 Again and again the Sayyid[1] made war and people helped him;
35 Thousand upon thousand, all with white turbans, he brought to the battle of Beerḍiga,
36 But what brought his downfall was the day when he destroyed the Khayr people.
37 Oh men, pride brings disaster: let that be remembered!

* * * * *

38 I saw a man such as those described who will not live long to enjoy his wealth,
39 He is full, satiated, and has grown fat buttocks like a big ram,

40 His bags are full of loot taken from men of honour and valour.
41 Watch silently, Muslims, and see how those who prosper lose their souls!

11. *The Looted Necklace*

ANONYMOUS

As has been seen already, the composition and recitation of poetry plays an important role in disputes and their settlement. In this group of poems three men and their kinsmen express their accusations, claims, and counter-claims in the form of a series of *gabays*. Those concerned are: Waʿays Ḥirsi, a caravan trader of the Habar Awal clan from Berbera, his agent and protector amongst the Ogaadeen clan, and Mataan Ḥuseen, a warrior of a rival section of the same clan. The incident which links these three men is the looting of Waʿays's caravan on its way from the coast of Berbera inland through the territory of the Ogaadeen about 1880. This involved not only Waʿays himself, but inevitably also his agents and protectors amongst the Ogaadeen, who were responsible for the safety and security of Waʿays's property. It was their duty to seek the return of the stolen goods, if necessary by force. Waʿays's losses included a decorative necklace, called *labahal*, which was formerly worn by men of substance and distinction, but which is now no longer in fashion. It is above all his loss of this necklace which Waʿays laments in lines 17 and 19.

As will be apparent, the attack on Waʿays's caravan by Mataan and his kinsmen was directed not at Waʿays particularly, but at

[1] In this line the poet attributes the ultimate downfall of the Dervish movement to the Sayyid's wanton attack on the Khayr section of the Ḍulbahante clan. This lineage is composed largely of men of religion whom Somali consider to be under Divine Protection.

34 Kaakici wadaadkii dagaal   Lagu na kaalmee ye

35 Kuman iyo lag wada duub cad   buu keenay Beerdhiga e

36 Wach se kabaalki jabay maalintuu   kariyay Reer Khayr e

37 Ragow, kibirka waa Lagu kufaa   kaa ha La ogaado!

* * * * *

38 Nin kuwaa ka dhigan baan arkay aan   kadab u noolayn e
39 Intoo uu kashbacay oo dhergay oo   kaman wan weyn yeeshay
40 Yuu niman karaamiyo col ba leh   kiish ka buuchsaday e
41 Ka shib dhaha, Islaameey, naftii   kii ladnaa gaday e!

his protectors and was designed to humiliate them and bring their power into disrepute. Mataan's lineage thus sought to challenge the authority of Waʿays's protectors whose leader had recently died (lines 1 and 2). In the event, all Waʿays's looted stock was recovered by the prompt action of his protectors (lines 12–13, 22–23), except for his cherished necklace. This Mataan held on to, but after some time sent a message to Waʿays inviting the latter to visit him and his people on his way back to the coast. Waʿays accepted and led his caravan to Mataan's camps where he was entertained with great hospitality. A fat camel, apparently, was slaughtered in Waʿays's honour, and Mataan recited the verse (lines 26–31) in which he explains his conduct and asks Waʿays to accept the return of his necklace. Thus the matter ended.

I. *Waʿays's lament*

1 Alas, authority is shaken, the royal lineage could not save us.
2 Had that great man lived, none would have dared harm us.
3 Only the meanest creature would travel such a (weary) road.
4 Those of my own age now weave back and forth in battle,
5 And now they are sending scouts out to the valleys of Herer.
6 While my young dun-coloured camels are driven slowly home,
7 And Deero and Laan are filling full the milking pails,[1]
8 And my senior wife Dahabo shuts the draughts from out of the house.
9 Am I waiting here to be killed; stock are like the growing grass.[2]

II. *The protector's reply*

10 Your words, Waʿays, are meaningless plaints wrung from your soul by fear.
11 Remember that these ill-spoken words will be carried to Herer,
12 Where your camels already stand penned by the lake;
13 Nor did we lay down our arms until what was yours had been recovered.

III. *Waʿays's rejoinder*

14 Was not my property attacked as it lay safe and hidden?
15 Did not each of those who came seize cloth apiece?

[1] *Deero* and *Laan* are names of camels.

[2] This phrase expresses the extent to which the nomad is dependent on his livestock for survival, and perhaps also the transitory nature of riches.

I

1 Dawlooy be'eey Reer Ugaas   naLagu dayn waa ye
2 Hadduu duubigii noolyahaan   naLa danqaabeen e
3 Dagdagle iyo nin diihaal qabaa   dawga soo mara e
4 Immikay da'daydii rogaal   daba maraysaa ye
5 Immikay ilaalada u diri   doochyadii Herer e
6 Immikaa nirgaha Loo dalqamin   dayrcadkaan dhaqay e

7 Immikaa markaha Laga dafsiin   Deero iyo Laan e
8 Immikay min weyn soo dugsiyi   Dahabadaydii ye

9 Dil miyaan ku sugi, choolo waa   doogga soo bachay e

II

10 Hal aad tidhi Wacaysow naf baa   Kaa halaanhalin e

11 Oo hee dheh, Herer waa La geyn   hadalchumaantaas e

12 Waa tay haleeladu dartaa   haro ku oodnayd e
13 Hubka maannu dhigin jeerohoon   helay wachaagii ye

III

14 Moodkayga oo dedan miyaan   weerar Lagu miisin?
15 Meeshii intii timid miyaan   maro maro u qaadan?

16 Were not even the very last remnants taken and abused?
17 Was not my necklace worn brazenly in Garduur?
18 Was this Mataan with my beads round his neck too much for you?
19 Does the power of protection give way before a man who is girded for battle?
20 For (of course) that life is sweet I grant you,
21 And where terror dwells are not all men the same?

IV. *The protector's answer*

22 If our leader is dead, then there are others in his place;
23 Already I have made the lakes of Doollo a watering-place for your camels.
24 But debts of gratitude are never honoured; and (of course) you are of the scheming Isaaq clan.
25 Who could imagine what more you might want, unless perhaps town property?

V. *Mataan's explanation*

26 The five lineages of Bah Ḥawaadle are remote from each other in descent,[1]
27 So also the rump and neck yield meat of a different quality,
28 Had I not sought to show how empty were the pledges of certain people, I should not have molested you.
29 And if the two of us had been partners the matter would not have turned out ill.
30 Your necklace is indeed beautiful, and I enjoyed my share of its splendour.
31 But now I surrender it to you: in God's justice take it!

12. *The Unpaid Bridewealth*

SALAAN ʿARRABEY

After many years spent in travel and work away from his home Salaan ʿArrabey returned to Somaliland and settled in one of the towns. Here, in his old age, he married a young girl and while following the Muslim marriage contract, scornfully refused to pay

[1] 'The five lineages of Bah Ḥawaadle' includes both the kinsmen of Waʿays's protector and those of their rival Mataan, and forms an important subdivision of the Ogaadeen clan.

16 Murqofkii ka soo hadhay miyaan — Lagu muraadaysan?
17 Ma makaawigaygaan Garduur — Lala mushaachaynin?
18 Ma Mataankan chidhan baan dartii — Loogu mari waayin?
19 Nin majiirta oo kaca miyaan — magane Loo waayin?

20 Naftu inay macaantahay anaa — Kuu markhaati yah e
21 Meeshii mildhaawe leh rag sow kula — masaal ma aha e?

IV

22 Hadduu duubigii lumay rag baa — degelladii yaal e
23 Waa taan dar chidhan Kaaga dhigay — harada Doollood e
24 Dad abaal ma gudo wachaad se tahay — dagayow Iidoor e
25 Wachaad dooni een daar ahayn — duga e yaa sheega?

V

26 Shanta reer e Bah Chawaadle waa — kala shisheeyaan e

27 Ha yeeshee shaf iyo gawrac way — kala shishlaadaan e
28 Rag baan sharad ku beenaynayee — ku ma shiddeeyeen e

29 Labadeenna oo shaariknaan — shuqul chumaadeen e

30 Hadday sharaf lahaayeen beryaan — soo shafeecsaday e

31 Adaan shayadii Kuu huree — sharac Allee qaado!

the additional Somali bridewealth. This disregard of the traditional Somali marriage custom he justified on two main grounds. Firstly because in an earlier marriage with a girl of the Ḍulbahante clan (line 21) he had paid an extortionate bridewealth, and secondly because he was now an old and broken man of small means. It is primarily as a lament on old age that this poem is remembered and recited today. The use of English words such as 'lecture' (line 5) and 'loafer' (lines 10 and 33) and other remarks in the poem reflect Salaan ʿArrabey's experiences in his travels.

1 Oh Faaraḥ, I had no desire to take up again the toils of poetry;
2 I had abandoned the travail of reciting importunate nonsense,
3 Although I am as skilled as any lawyer in the art of alliteration, be it the letter L or B,
4 Indeed I was taught on a wooden tablet by my grandfather who made me strong in the art.
5 Some people recite words as foolish and nonsensical as the European's 'lectures'
6 And still keep at it imagining themselves successful,
7 But the lines which I intone will be taken up and chanted after me.
8 Once sincerity and honour are left behind poetry is broken-tongued.
9 When a man reaches the age of twenty he wrestles with the world,
10 If I was once a 'loafer' now I am a decrepit old man,
11 A man whose hair is streaked with grey like the strands of a rope and broken to burdens,
12 By twelve years I have exceeded sixty; and this is certain.
13 My backbone and my body have slackened and my arms have lost their swagger,
14 Last night I had no sleep for pain and moaning,
15 Indeed my eyes peer blinking, and my sight is feeble,
16 I shake like something trembling in the wind.
17 Even as a she-camel which has been milked dry in the rainless season will not yield much milk,
18 So is he who treats distant relatives as though they were his clansmen.
19 Whenever I handed over a portion of my bridewealth it was consumed at once,

1 Luukaansi gabay Faarachow — laaki ma lahayn e

2 Laflaf iyo lahwiga Loo tirshiyo — jaray lurkiisii ye
3 La'da charafka laankiyo ba'daan — looyar ku ahay e

4 Nin awowgi looch ugu dhigoo — liil geshaan ahay e

5 Lagjar Ferenji niman baa akhriya — laawis iyo been e

6 Oo weli ba laasima intay — lib is ku moodaan e
7 Anse wachaan u laaqimahayaa — tichay ku luuqshaan e

8 Mar hadduu lillaahida ka bacho — waa lisaan jaban e

9 Nin labaatan buuchsaday adduun — waa legdamayaan e

10 Haddaan anigu loofari iqiin — haatan lowlabay e
11 Nin cirradu lammaanaa dhigtay oo — laylyan baan ahay e

12 Lichdan labiyo toban baan kor maray — waa na La hubaa ye
13 Lafta dhabar lachaadka i debciyo — laafyihii gacanta

14 Lubbidaydu layl chalay ma ledin — laadadyiyo taah e
15 Waa taa lanleemada indhaa — araggu liitaa ye
16 Liiqliiqad baan ahay sidii — lulo dabayleed e
17 Ma lichiibto geela ba hashii — lahantay jiilaal e

18 Ku laabudan shisheeye na ninkii — lachawsi moodaa ye

19 Had ba wachaan lacaaf riday rag baa — laastay yaradkii ye

20 And if tonight you want to milk me I will be dry.
21 The Ḍulbahante clan used me to their advantage and took me for a fool,
22 I dissipated my property while they despised me,
23 In my vanity I brought this loss upon myself;
24 Wisdom eludes a careless man and people do not trust him;
25 A solidly woven rope of two strands holds fast even when it is worn to a thread,
26 Some threads always remain of a drawing rope which was once supple and strong.
27 If once pride held my head erect now my back is bent;
28 However much manliness men claim, time will grind them down;
29 Often it is a trifling matter which brings you down.
30 I am not of the same age as you of the younger generation which is without depth.
31 I still regret in my heart my former extravagance towards my wife's relatives;
32 I am still sick with the pain and nausea of it.
33 He who in his youth was a loafer ever pursues what he missed.
34 With clansmen who are your flesh you must seek reconciliation as strong as a bone.
35 The addition of a decorative cape and a saddle always increases the value of a horse,
36 When men joust and wrestle in battle, and the dust rises,
37 A young horse which does not know the saddle is disobedient to the guiding thigh of the rider.
38 A healthy young man like you cannot know the sickness which I endure;
39 It is you who should come with a burden-camel laden with mats or bring its equivalent;
40 I hate those who come empty-handed, carrying a long herding stick;
41 Oh brother-in-law! Do not tire your legs in vain; it is shameful to hanker after gifts.

20 Labchan maayo caawa na haddaad   lis i tidhaahdaan e
21 Liibaan Dhulbahantaa iga helay   laalluf se i mood ye

22 Chaqaygaan ku laacibay hadday   igu lihiimeen e
23 Sidaan ugu lallabay waaniga   laayacays baday e
24 Nin laqwiyay tashigu waa ka lali   Lagu na leecaan ye
25 Lammadaade chadhig Loo tidcay   lugi ka doogtaa ye

26 Lufan baa ka hadha dawliskii   liilsamaan jiray e

27 Haddaan luqunta beri taagi jiray   liicday adhachdii ye
28 Nin laboonti sheegta ba sabaan   laarriyaa heli ye

29 Chaajada liciifkii aday   Kuu lad noqotaa ye
30 La fil ma ihi laankiin dambaan   duchi lillaynayn e

31 Laqantooyo chidid tii horaan   laabta ku hayaa ye

32 Imminkaan ladhkii weli qabaa   liqanyadeedii ye
33 Nin yaraan ku loofaray wuchuu   lumiyay raacdee ye

34 Tol lachmi yah ladqabo waw egtay   inaad lafaysaa ye

35 Fardaha ba libaadshaha iyo duntaa   ladha waliidkood e

36 Rag laacdamaya lool iyo rogaal   leechada is goysay
37 Bawdada ma laasimo darmaan   leeddafuul ihi ye

38 Laajeertidaan qabo barbaar   ladani waa moog e

39 Adigaan lamma'o awr leh wadin   amma liggood keenin

40 Leegleegsadaa waa nebcay   laanta dheer sida e

41 Seeddow ha igu soo lug go'in   lahasho waa ceeb e!

13. *Ingratitude*

SALAAN ʿARRABEY

This poem was composed while Salaan ʿArrabey was in Nairobi. The poet was destitute at the time and looked for help from a well-off cousin living in Nairobi upon whom he had himself showered kindnesses in the past. In the poem Salaan ʿArrabey complains of this kinsman's ingratitude, claiming that not only did he give no help himself, and denied his debt, but also counselled other members of the Somali community in Nairobi to take no notice of Salaan's plight. Three specific occasions of Salaan's goodness to his cousin are recalled in the poem. First, the poet's intervention on his cousin's behalf in a dispute between their clan and the Ḍulbahante clan. The ungrateful cousin had been captured by the Ḍulbahante and was only released when Salaan summoned many of his clansmen to his help with considerable difficulty (lines 1–12). Amongst other things, this required the conciliation of an internal feud amongst the Nuuḥ Maḥammed lineage referred to in line 8. A further consequence of this incident was the arrest of his cousin by the Government, when Salaan again intervened successfully on his behalf (lines 28–30).

Secondly, the poet recalls his part in the battle of Faayo Wood when an attempt was made to recover camels looted from his cousin by another clan (lines 33–40). Thirdly, Salaan refers to his successful recovery of his cousin's bride who had been abducted and whom his cousin had not succeeded in rescuing (lines 43–48). In the poem these episodes are connected by a continuous plaint.

1 (I sing of) the man on whose behalf I shouted for help until my lungs were dry,
2 For whom I ran with shoulders bent until I was completely without breath,
3 And for whom I anxiously raised the rallying cry 'Habar Ḥabuusheed'[1] until people mistook me for a nightjar,
4 And on account of whom my skin itched from my rapid passage through the *jillab*[2] grass,
5 And as I made my way through the night I fell and tore myself on *hagar*[3] bushes.
6 Like the Ethiopians in attack, a mass of warriors,
7 Numerous as you know, I assembled for him;

[1] Habar Ḥabuusheed is a collective name for the Habar Tol Jaʿlo clan, recording their descent through a woman of Ethiopian origin.

[2] A species of *Indigofera*.

[3] A species of *Commiphora*.

1 Qaylada chaduurki ninkay charaqday laabtaydu

2 Chusulduubka orodkii ninkaan dhab ugu chuurtoobay

3 Ayaa Habar Chabuushaay ninkii chiidka La i mooday

4 Jillabkii chadhaadhaa ninkaan ugu chajiimooday

5 Guuraa chambaarada ninkii chagarku ii jeechay

6 Guutada chamaaska ah sidii Chabasha duullaan ah
7 Chaddigaa ogaydeen, ninkaan chaadir uga yeelay

8 For his sake I made peace amongst the generous Nuuḥ Maḥammed (and summoned their aid);
9 In the thickets of Odayaḍeero when the warriors were so locked in battle that they touched each others' testicles,
10 When the unholy Olol swore by his wife (not to give way),
11 Then I seized my weapons and rushed forward like the winged hornbill
12 And in this conflict with the alien foe gave no quarter.
13 (But he is like) women distraught in the pangs of labour,
14 Who, since their memories are short, have forgotten the pain when their menses come again.
15 Let him disregard his bounden duty to me, and fail to aid me with his strength;
16 But amazing is the wickedness of he who disclaims great deeds wrought for his sake.

* * * * *

17 Dhows cannot sail in the calm lull before the Karan season;[1]
18 Kindling is necessary to set ablaze a log of wood;

19 A horse begins to rebel against his bridle when mishandled;

20 In a deserted place I sit in desolation like a vulture on the Guban plains,
21 Yet I would have been successful in the game[2] had I not lacked support.

* * * * *

22 The disputing elders reach an unjust decision.
23 When men debate face to face and the issue becomes clear

24 The tongue is like a sword cutting off life.

25 There are men who keep no record of their dues and they are sent to make trouble behind our backs.

* * * * *

26 In both wisdom and oratory I am fully accomplished;
27 I am a man whose words judges quote, and excellent in every respect.

* * * * *

[1] A short rain season falling in July and August.

[2] 'The game' corresponds here to the Somali word *ḥeego*, which is a Somali version of hockey; here: 'the game of life'.

8 Childhibaanka Nuuch Machammedkaan   kala chadhkaynaayay
9 Chidhkii Odaya-Dheerood markii   rag is chiniin taabtay

10 Charaamigii Olol markuu   chila fur kaw siiyay
11 Waa taan u chuubsaday sidii   chuurta baalka leh e

12 Charbigii shisheeyaa ninkaan   cheebashada diiday
13 Dumarku ba chublada foosha waa   chanaf wareeraa ye
14 Bal se inay chusuus daranyihiin   chaylka kale moog e

15 Wachba yaanu cheerkay i marin   choog na ii furan e

16 Chaasha e, nin libin Kaa chistiyay   chumihi waa yaab e

* * * * *

17 Doonyuhu chawaal ku ma socdaan   cheelli karameed e
18 Hadduu chanan yar yara leeyahay buu   cholod hulaaqaa ye
19 Faras na wuchuu chakamadiid noqdaa   kol uu charraamaa ye
20 Cidluun baan chayuugnahay sidii   chunshadii Guban e
21 Cheegada haddaan dhalin lahaa   choogmadaan ahay e

* * * * *

22 Cheerbeegti murantaa gartay   cheelli hadashaa ye
23 Chubin rag is ku waajahay hadday   chayga ka caddaato
24 Afku wuchuu la chawl yahay magliga   chawda Kaa jara e
25 Rag uun baan chisaabta na oqoon   chin na Loo diray e

* * * * *

26 Chikaayo iyo baane ba anaan   charaf i seegayn e
27 Nin chukaantu wada naadiso oo   chaadsadaan ahay e

* * * * *

28 The man for whom I went to such lengths in the District Office
29 And secured his prompt release from the prison of the enemy,
30 And even, when the time to pay his blood-dues came, paid for him from my own camels,
31 Let him disregard his bounden duty to me, and fail to aid me with his strength;
32 But amazing is the wickedness of he who disclaims great deeds wrought for his sake.

* * * * *

33 Confronted by a forest of enemy clansmen at the battle of Faayo Wood,
34 When the she-camel called Ḥiito cried with fear, to avenge the audacious raid upon your camels
35 For your sake I harried the enemy champion, envious Buqul.

36 That time when I came out of the battle brandishing my sword, Ḥaashi will remember,
37 Your closest kin the Bah Reer Dood did nothing to help you,

38 Your life was not yet finished when already the death cry had gone up,
39 That I did not abandon you then the clan knows well.
40 And Ḥasan Nuur is a witness to this, that time when men were girding up their robes (for battle).
41 Let him disregard his bounden duty to me, and fail to aid me with his strength;
42 But amazing is the wickedness of he who disclaims great deeds wrought for his sake.

* * * * *

43 The men with whom I was allied since the time of Adam and Eve
44 Whose friendship I had worked hard to win, the Reer Jibriil, were forced to act according to the circumstances;
45 And now there is no cheerful banter between us, no mirth of life,
46 With that Qasaal who stole your betrothed, Ḥaddiyo, you were at enmity,
47 And although you were both equal in lineage he made you a woman,

28 Chafiiskii magaalada wichii   chaalad igu gaadhay

29 Chabsigii cadaawaa ninkaan   chaalan uga saaray
30 Choolaa muggay timi ninkaan   chulayay geelayga

31 Wachba yaanu cheerkay i marin   choog na i furan e

32 Chaasha e, nin libin Kaa chistiyay   chumihi waa yaab e

* * * * *

33 Choontii walaalaa ahayd   Chodayadii Faayo

34 Charragaqaadkii Suub markay   Chiito ololaysay

35 Dartaa baan chanaaq ugu lurriyay   Chaasidkii Buqul e
36 Chawdheerta goortaan la bachay   Chaashi bay garan e

37 Bah Reer Dood chigtay Kuu ahayd   Ku ma se chaalayn e
38 Chinjirtaan wafoobin e kolkii   chuurtu kor u yeedhdhay

39 Chisti inaanan Kaa gelin tolkaan   chog ina moogayn e
40 Chasan Nuur na way marag kolkii   rag is u chaydnaa ye
41 Wachba yaanu cheerkay i marin   choog na ii furan e

42 Chaasha e, nin libin Kaa chistiyay   chumihi waa yaab e

* * * * *

43 Nimankaan channaanada lahayn   Haawa iyo Aadan

44 Chigaalkaan tabcaday Reer Jibriil   charawigii raac ye
45 Waayadan chayaad La ma kaftamo   chaashir nololeed e
46 Qasaalkii Chaddiyo Kaa dhacay baad   chinif lahaydeen e
47 Chuska dhalasho waa Kula sinnaa   chilo se Kaa yeel ye

48 But when I attacked him with my sharp sword his pride was tamed;
49 Remember that by yourself you could not have brought her home,
50 And I who restored your honour you seek to slander.

* * * * *

51 People know me for a wise man and honour and respect me
52 And when I go to the coast people offer thanks to God,
53 (Or if I am absent) men watch the stars as anxiously as they foretell the arrival of the Ḥays rains[1]

* * * * *

54 Kinsmen should be as the thorn fence protecting the encampment.
55 When misfortune seized me—and the Lord's decrees fall immutably upon us—
56 (Why did you not) shout until you were hoarse, summoning a thousand men to my aid?
57 Let him disregard his bounden duty to me, and fail to aid me with his strength;
58 But amazing is the wickedness of he who disclaims great deeds wrought for his sake.

* * * * *

59 The good name of the noble-minded is besmirched by the loose talk of fools.
60 You have desecrated the love which I have shown you,

61 By God, if there was any generosity in me for you, you have destroyed it;
62 But those whom a man befriends hate him in secret.

* * * * *

63 The veins on my neck are swollen, my tendons stick out,
64 My ribs are stiff, and my bones bereft of flesh,
65 And my skin which was once like silk has lost its beauty;
66 Now I am as decrepit as a worn-out burden-camel.
67 With your two hands you eagerly took my fresh first milk, my fresh milk was taken.

* * * * *

[1] A short rain season falling between December and January.

48 Chiiraaga goortaan la dhacay   chaasil kibirkii ye

49 Ogoobey, Chiddaayadii dartaa   ku ma cherowdeen e

50 Ninkaygii chorta ba Kaa dhigaad   chimi tidhaahdaa ye

* * * * *

51 Chidaar baa halqigu ii yaqaan   chay iyo maamuus e
52 Chamdu baa ba La ii wada naqaa   cheeb haddaan tago e
53 Sida chayska roobkaa nafluu   ii chiddigiyaa ye

* * * * *

54 Ooddu ba chirsiga reerka waa   bilichijaabtaa ye

55 Haddii aniga Lay chidho Rabbaa   chugunki meel yaal e

56 Adigoo chabeebsaday intaad   kun igu chaydaanto

57 Wachba yaanu cheerkay i marin   choog na i furan e

58 Chaasha e, nin libin Kaa chistiyay   chumihi waa yaab e

* * * * *

59 Chintifaallo doqoneed nin rag ah   waa chasariyaa ye

60 Chubbaddaan idiin dhaqanayaad   igu chujayseen e
61 Allaylee, churmo haddaan lahaa   waygu chilateen e

62 Rag ba se kii aad charadhaamiso yaa   Kuu chasaas col ah e

* * * * *

63 Chawlalmariiddada mergiga   chididdadays oojay
64 Feedhaa chidhiidhsamay lafaa   chuubku ka idlaaday
65 Jidhkaygii chariirta u ekaa   chaadhuf quruchdii ye
66 Hadduun baan charaarugay sidii   chamilgab awryaal e
67 Chafto inaydin ii labalisteen   choochdii La i maal ye

* * * * *

68 If in this life we failed to find love from each other
69 In the next world the Lord will judge and give us our just portion.
70 Now I commit you to your fate, and fasten it to your robe,

71 (In the circle of kinsmen round you) let someone else stand in my place, for I renounce all ties with you.

14. *Oh Clansmen, Stop the War!*

SALAAN ʿARRABEY

This poem was recited to stop a war between two closely connected lineages of the Habar Tol Jaʿlo clan, the Aḥmed and Daahir Faaraḥ, when in pursuance of an old feud these groups were about to attack each other. Salaan ʿArrabey took up position in a valley between the rival encampments on the eve of the impending engagement and addressed them in the words of the poem. He was heard by the sentries who summoned the leaders of each party and they listened to his words, which apparently prevented the battle from developing. The relationships of the two groups and of the poet himself which are important for an understanding of the poem are shown in the skeleton genealogy:

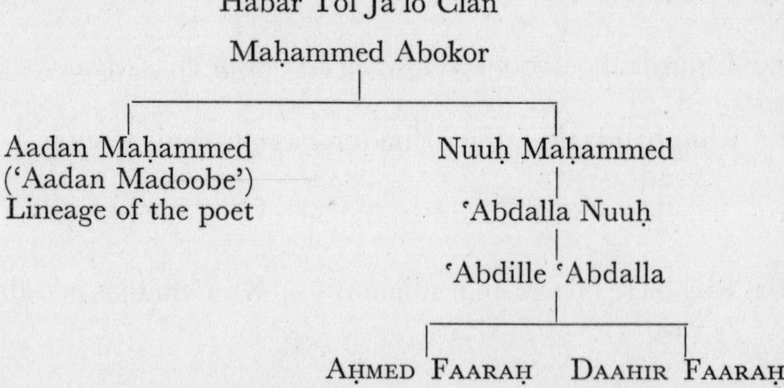

In general the poet seeks to stop the two hostile parties by convincing them of the evils of war and particularly of war amongst closely related groups of the same clan. Thus he refers to the battles of ʿAloolaʿad (line 3) and ʿAnla (line 27), when closely related sections of his clan (the Habar Tol Jaʿlo) cut each other to pieces, and also to a number of internecine sporadic killings (lines 28–36). He further mentions the battle of Meygaag ʿIidan (line 4) where a similarly disastrous engagement took place amongst related sections of the Ḍulbahante clan. The poet appeals to the rival Aḥmed and

68 Ifka intaynu chay nahay haddaan chiiso kala weynay
69 Aakhiro Rabbaa ina chukumi chaqa inoo yaal e

70 Imminkaan nabsiga Kugu chawilay chaynka Kuu sudhan e
71 Chaggaygii wach dhigo haatanaan Kaa chaliil jabay e!

Daahir Faaraḥ sections to recall how often prosperity leads to overweening pride, pride to war, and war to famine and disaster. This occurs at lines 9–14, lines 42–52, and again at lines 61–74, where the poet points to the reduced power and prestige of the Majeerteen clan (particularly of the ʿIsmaan Maḥamuud, ʿIgadle and ʿIise sections), and their impoverished state, again the result of internal schisms.

Finally, it should perhaps be noted that the poem's reputed success in averting bloodshed may be as much due to the poet's threat to intervene with his lineage on one side (lines 38–40), as to the effect of his words.

1 The day the ʿUmar Daahir
2 Cut themselves to pieces in the battle
3 Of ʿAloolaʿad, he who was present then
4 And who also knows what happened at the battle of Meygaag ʿIidan,
5 Knows to the full
6 The horror and the turmoil (of war)
7 And understands its real nature;
8 Oh clansmen, stop the war!

* * * * *

9 He who sups plentifully every night
10 (Whom pride and prosperity shroud like) shadeless cloud
11 And damp mist mixed together,
12 That in his good fortune
13 He should repose in peace and tranquillity
14 Would be hard to credit.
15 Oh clansmen, stop the war!

* * * * *

16 The tenour of my words
17 He whose leaf of life has withered[1]
18 And the slow-witted fool will not understand;
19 But when (the warriors) die in countless number
20 And the great array of men is utterly destroyed
21 People will soon reproach each other;
22 Oh clansmen, stop the war!

* * * * *

[1] There is an old tradition that on the moon there is a tree, each leaf of which represents a man's life. And when this leaf withers and falls, the man whose fate is tied to the leaf will die forty days later.

1 Maalintii Cumar Daahir
2 Is ku gooyay cayaartiyo
3 Nin Caloolacad joogay
4 Oo Meygaag Ciiden war qaatay

5 Waa cibaaro qabaa yoo
6 Belaayuu curufkeediyo
7 Camalkeeda yaqaan e
8 Waar tolow, colka jooja!

* * * * *

9 Nin habeenno casheeyay
10 Cadar aan hadh lahayn
11 Iyo ceeryaamays ugu toosta
12 Oo inuu caafiyaddiisa
13 Cabbaar meel la fadhiisto
14 Caqligaanay gelayn e
15 Waar tolow, colka jooja!

* * * * *

16 Carrabkaan ku hadlaayo na
17 Nin caleenti caddaatiyo
18 Caamadaan garanayn oo
19 Kolkay cuurar dhintaan e
20 Cutub weyni cidlaataa
21 Lays canaanan had dhow e
22 Waar tolow, colka jooja!

* * * * *

23 You two lineages,
24 Hurling boasts of strength in each other's teeth;
25 We are more tightly bound as kinsmen than any other group
26 And yet there is rancour amongst us.
27 We remember the battle of ʿAnla
28 And the five (we lost); amongst them ʿAadle
29 And the first-born son of my mother
30 And ʿAli Fiin, we have not forgotten,
31 And those killed in a desolate place
32 Were kinsmen to us,
33 And Jaamaʿ, loved by all
34 And our leading spokesman,
35 And Rabjaan, both in revelry
36 And in defiance of our custom you killed,
37 And now if you start to devour each other
38 I will not stand aloof
39 But adding my strength to one side
40 I shall join in the attack on the other.
41 Oh clansmen, stop the war!

* * * * *

42 No sooner had ʿAntar's pride[1] swelled within you
43 When prosperity overflowed its brink,
44 Than your corpses lay piled upon each other
45 And the foul hyena
46 And the birds of prey tore at them in the sands;
47 And after your deliverance from those bitter straits
48 The fresh, green grass of Balanbaal
49 And the pastures of Karamaan
50 And ʿAyn, you exhausted;
51 And no camels bearing young were left
52 And no homesteads filled with sheep and goats remained;
53 Oh clansmen, stop the war!

* * * * *

54 With men like children and the weak,
55 With fools who sit in the homesteads,
56 Proudly posturing in the assembly place,

1 'ʿAntar's pride swelled within you', lit. 'You became like ʿAntar'. ʿAntara bin Shaddaad (also known as ʿAntar) was a famous warrior of the pre-Islamic period in Arabia.

23 Labadiinnatan cuur e
24 Is u coobe ridaayow
25 Cid na ways u chignaa
26 Ciil na ways u qabnaa
27 Canla na waa is ogayn
28 Shantii Caadle lahayd
29 Iyo curadkii habartay iyo
30 Cali Fiin ma illaawin
31 Oo raggii ceeriga yiilla
32 Casabaannu ahayn
33 Oo Jaamacii calmanaa ye
34 Codkar noogu horreeyiyo
35 Rabjaan baydin cayaayir
36 Iyo caado dhaaf ku disheen
37 Oo haddii aad is cuntaan
38 Idin caabudan maayo
39 Oo waa intaan mid la ciidmi
40 Oo ka kaleeto ku ciiri ye
41 Waar tolow, colka jooja!

* * * * *

42 Intii baad Cantarteen oo
43 Cunkadaydin marteen
44 Oo meydkiinnii cammirraa ye
45 Candhadheerta dhurwaa
46 Iyo ciidda haaddu ku jiidday
47 Iyo cuqduudkii ka bachdeen
48 Oo cosobkii Balanbaal
49 Iyo caleentii Karamaan
50 Iyo Cayn baa soo gudhsateen
51 Oo cambartii geela dhalaysiyo
52 Adhaa ceegan guryaa e
53 Waar tolow, colka jooja!

* * * * *

54 Nin carruur iyo maato
55 Iyo calli reero la yaal
56 Oo is coofaaya golaa

57 Who would run for safety with speed,
58 And with men who counsel war
59 And are determined on it, you are full;
60 Oh clansmen, stop the war!

* * * * *

61 (Just as) the Majeerteen clan their glory,
62 And their tribute from the Hawiye people
63 And their regal staff,[1] have lost,
64 The ʽIsmaan Maḥamuud lineage
65 And ʽIgalle's descendants who are in the same plight
66 And ʽIise's people, are all deficient in strength;
67 In the regions of ʽAdduun
68 And ʽAdaale they pasture no longer,
69 At ʽAsayr and Sayn
70 By the famous tree
71 Beyond ʽAwbarre
72 In remote places
73 Facing the shore
74 They are forced to turn for sustenance to the fruit of the immature date palm.
75 And this is the path you are following (to the same end)
76 Oh clansman, stop the war!

15. *The Limits of Submission*

FAARAḤ NUUR

This poem describes how the poet's clan had for long lived in submission to a stronger group, but were driven in the end to rebel and to assert their independence.

1 Over and over again to people
2 I show abundant kindness.

* * * * *

3 If they are not satisfied
4 I spread out bedding for them
5 And invite them to sleep.

* * * * *

[1] 'Regal staff' refers to the decorated wooden staff of office traditionally carried by some clan sultans.

Oo cararaaya had dhow
Iyo nin colaad talinaaya
Oo caddaystaydinka buucha e
Waar tolow, colka jooja!

*　*　*　*　*

Majeerteen calankii
Iyo cashuurtii Hawiyaa
Iyo cukaaskii boqor waa
Oo Reer Cismaan Machamuud
Iyo Cigallii ka dhignaa
Iyo Ciise ways ku itaal
Iyo in dhowayd ba Cadduun
Iyo Cadaale reer ma furayn
Casaasayr iyo Sayn iyo
Geedkii caanka ahaa
Iyo Cawbaarrawgu sokaysa
Oo hadduu cawtalgasiira
Iyo badda coonka u jeedda
Ka cawaaganayaa

Oo caynkii baydin waddaan e
Waar tolow, colka jooja!

Rag sabaan ka sabaan baan
Samaantuun badiyaa

*　*　*　*　*

Hadduu saakimi waayo
Sariiraan u dhigaa
Is ka seecho idhaa

*　*　*　*　*

6 If they are still not satisfied,
7 The milk of the camel whose name is Suub
8 I milk three times for them,
9 And tell them to drink it up.

* * * * *

10 If they are still not satisfied,
11 The homestead's ram,
12 And the fat he-goat I kill for them.

* * * * *

13 If they are still not satisfied,
14 The plate from Aden
15 I fill with ghee for them.

* * * * *

16 If they are still not satisfied,
17 A beautiful girl
18 And her bridal house I offer them.

* * * * *

19 If they are still not satisfied,
20 I select livestock also
21 And add them to the tribute.

* * * * *

22 If they are still not satisfied,
23 'Oh brother-in-law, oh Sultan, oh King!'
24 These salutations I lavish upon them.

* * * * *

25 If they are still not satisfied,
26 At the time of early morning prayers I prepare
27 The dark grey horse with black tendons,
28 And with the words 'Praise to the Prophet' I take
29 The iron-shafted spear,
30 And drive it through their ribs
31 So that their lungs spew out;
32 Then they are satisfied!

Hadduu saakimi waayo na
Caanihii hasha Suub baan
Saddech goor u lisaa
Ku sarriigo idhaa

* * * * *

Hadduu saakimi waayo
Sumalkii rugta joogay iyo
Sogobkaan u qalaa

* * * * *

Hadduu saakimi waayo
Siirigii Cadameed baan
Subaggawga badshaa

* * * * *

Hadduu saakimi waayo
Gabadh suurad wanaagsan baan
Surradda ugu dhisaa

* * * * *

Hadduu saakimi waayo
Choolo gooni u soofiyo
Sadadaan ku ladhaa

* * * * *

Hadduu saakimi waayo
Seeddow, mood iyo mood iyo
Salaantaan badiyaa

* * * * *

Hadduu saakimi waayo
Salaaddaan lallabaa yoo
Meydal seedo madow iyo
Salligaan cuskadaa yoo
Sulub eebo ku joogtaan
Sarartaa ku dhuftaa
Sambabkaa ka bachshaa
Markaasuu sellimaa!

B · TRADITIONAL AND MODERN SONGS

16. *A Bridal Song Sung in Honour of a Bride*

ANONYMOUS

1 Great is your fortune, who went out to seek him for you?
2 Who told you of our boy, five times a man?

17. *Lament for a Dead Lover*

SIRAAD ḤAAD

1 You were the fence standing between our land and the descendants of ʿAli,
2 (Now in your departure) you are the sky which gives no rain while mist shrouds the world,
3 The moon that shines no more,
4 The risen sun extinguished,
5 The dates on their way from Basra cut off by the seas.

18. *A Woman Sings of Her Love*

ANONYMOUS

1 Oh, you are a kilt which a young dandy set out to choose,
2 Oh, you are like a costly ring for which thousands were paid,
3 Will I ever find your like—you who have been shown to me only once?
4 An umbrella comes apart; you are (as strong as) looped iron;
5 Oh, you (who are as) the gold of Nairobi, finely moulded,
6 You are the risen sun, and the early rays of dawn.
7 Will I ever find your like, you who have been shown to me only once?

1 Ayaan badaneey, ayaa Kuu ilaalo tegay?
2 Ayaa Kuu sheegay shan-ka-roone inankayaga?

1 Dalkeenniyo Reer Caloo deyr La kala marshow

2 Cirkoo di'i waayay oo dunidu ciirtayow

3 Dayacha nuurkiisa oon dib u iftiiminow
4 Shamsada oo daalacdoo Laga dam siiyayow
5 Basra timirtii ka imanaysay oo baddii chidhdhow

1 Subeeciyad wiil benderi baadhasho u tegow
2 Kaatun feyruusi yoo kuman La siiyayow
3 Miyaan masaalkaa helayaa, mar La i tusyow?

4 Dallaayadii waa jabtaa, biraha duubanow

5 Dahabka Nayroobi oo daacad Loo tumow
6 Shamsada oo soo bachdiyo shaaca waaberow
7 Miyaan masaalkaa helayaa, mar La i tusyow?

19. *Camel-Watering Chant*

ANONYMOUS

This is sung by kinsmen as they water their camels.

They are all here, ready,
They belong to us
How splendid and useful they are
And they are standing ready.

* * * * *

I set my foot (on the well),
Oh Master of the world,[1]
Oh God the Just, make our task easy.

* * * * *

You will be cooled,
Come forward slowly.

* * * * *

Put your mouth to it with blessing,
It is devoid of evil,
Your shrivelled bones,
Are now moist and full again.

* * * * *

When they are standing ready,
And the clansmen are all present,
None must leave till all are watered.

20. *Release*

ANONYMOUS

Oh girls I am held by a spirit,
If you have any love for me,
Cut from both my shoulders its torments and arrows!

[1] The phrase 'Master of the world' corresponds in the Somali text to '*Aalamiin*, a borrowing from Arabic where it means 'worlds'. The word occurs in the opening line of the First Sura of the Quran, which runs as follows: 'Glory be to God, the Master of the worlds'. The line is frequently used in prayers and pious ejaculations, but some Somalis in the nomadic interior have abbreviated it to its last component '*aalamiin*, and treat it simply as a praise name of God.

1 Waa tan oo timid
2 Waa na teennii
3 Waa na tolmoon
4 Waa na tubantahay

*   *   *   *

5 Cagta saaray e
6 Caalamiinkiyo
7 Caadilkow sahal

*   *   *   *

8 Waad qaboobi ye
9 Qun yar soo soco

*   *   *   *

10 Shifo ku af saar
11 Oo shar Kuu ma leh
12 Farihii kogay
13 Waa kuwa fiday

*   *   *   *

14 Hadday tubantahay
15 Ay tol leedahay
16 Loo ma kala tago

1 Hablow, saar baan qabaa
2 Haddaad gacal ii tihiin
3 Galiilyada labada garab iyo gantaalaha mayga goyn?

21. *Choice*

ANONYMOUS

Oh girls, insults and praise,
Sleep upon my stomach;
With which one have you fallen in love?
For which one shall I spread my grass bed?

22. *Fortitude*

ANONYMOUS

Like a she-camel with a large bell
Come from the plateau and upper Haud,
My heat is great.

* * * *

Birds perched together on the same tree
Call each their own cries,
Every country has its own ways,
Indeed people do not understand each others' talk.

* * * *

One of my she-camels falls on the road
And I protect its meat,
At night I cannot sleep,
And in the daytime I can find no shade.

* * * *

I have broken my nose on a stick,
I have broken my right hip,
I have something in my eye,
And yet I go on.

23. *Dance Hunger*

ANONYMOUS

I don't take any of the best meat,
I don't drink from a big vessel,
But I have a great appetite for dancing.

1 Hablow, cay iyo ammaan
2 Calooshayday hurdaan
3 Middee baa caashaqdeen?
4 Middeen cawda u goglaa?

1 Sidii koorweyn halaad oo
2 Kor iyo Hawd sare ka timid
3 Kulayl badan baan qabaa

* * * *

4 Shimbiro geed wada koraa
5 Midi ba cayn bay u cidaa
6 Carro ba waa camaladdeed
7 Illayn Lays ma cod yaqaan

* * * *

8 Hal baa hilin igaga jaban
9 Hilbaha yaan ka ceshadaa
10 Habeenkii ka ma lulmoodoo
11 Dharaartii ka ma hadh galo

* * * *

12 Sankaa qori igaga jabay
13 Sintaa midig baan ka jabay
14 Il baa sachar igaga dhacay
15 Haddana waan soconayaa

1 Cadka bawdo ka ma cuno
2 Caanaha na doobi ka ma dhamo
3 Sacab se waw cir weynahay

24. *A Wish*

ANONYMOUS

1 You who are like the holy water which the pilgrims bring from Mecca, like a lantern;
2 You are like stone sugar;
3 Oh Lord, how I wish I could swallow you!

25. *The Dancer's Needs*

ANONYMOUS

1 Unless I marry a wife who has been married before,
2 Unless I eat her sweet-meats,
3 I will not have the strength to lift my foot in dance.

26. *The Best Dance*

ANONYMOUS

1 The best dance is the dance of the Eastern clans,
2 The best people are ourselves,
3 Of this I have always been sure.
4 The best wealth is camels,
5 The *duur*[1] grass is the best fresh grazing,
6 The *dareemo*[2] grass is the best hay,
7 Of this I have always been sure.

27. *Twelve Modern Love Songs*

ANONYMOUS

These are modern love songs of the towns typical of those broadcast today by radio and widely listened to even in the interior of the country. The last three are connected with the life of medical dressers and dispensers who, like lorry drivers, are particularly given

[1] A species of *Andropogon*.

[2] A species of *Chrysopogon*.

Samsam iyo siraad u egeey

Sonkor dhagach sideedii
Rabbow, yaa siiba oo liqa?

Carmal guursadaa mooyee
Cadriyadda cunaa mooyee
Cagta soo ma rogi karo

Sacab inuu Dad Bari yahay
Dad na inuu annaga yahay
Awal ba waw dareen qabay
Inay duunyo geel tahay
Duur inuu caleen yahay
In dareemo caws tahay
Awal ba waw dareen qabay

to this form of verse. The popular form of modern song was indeed, as was mentioned already, devised by a lorry driver some twenty years ago.

I

1 The oryx does not bring her young into the open,
2 Why are you doing this with your thigh?

II

1 A flash of lightning does not satisfy thirst,
2 What then is it to me if you just pass by?

III

1 It is the custom of the Somali,
2 To mock a man who has fallen in love.

IV

1 One does not hurry past a dying man,
2 Before I enter the grave, spare a word for me.

V

1 When you die you will enter the earth,
2 Let not the preacher then turn you from your love-song.

VI

1 Is it lightning far distant from me,
2 That I have strained for vainly?

VII

1 The girl for whom I have withered like a stick,
2 Are you telling me to despair of ever attaining?

VIII

1 My heart is single and cannot be divided,
2 And it is fastened on a single hope; Oh you who might be the moon.

IX

1 Until I die I shall not give up the love-song,
2 Oh God, forgive me my shortcomings.

I

1 Biciidku dhashiisa bannaan ma dhigo e
2 Machaad u bannaysaa bawdadaa?

II

1 Hillaac bilig yidhi harraad ma ba'sho e
2 Muchuu hormarkaagu ii tari?

III

1 Soomaaliday caadadeed tahay
2 Nin caashaqay bay ku caydaa

IV

1 Ninkii dhimanaya La ma dhaafo e
2 Intaanan dhulka gelin wach uun i dheh

V

1 Haddii aad dhimato na dhul baad geliyeey
2 Wadaad yuu Ku dhaafin dhaantaada e

VI

1 Hillaac aan ii dhowayn
2 Ma hallabsaday e?

VII

1 Yartaan u qallalay sidii qori
2 Ka quuso miyaad i leedahay?

VIII

1 Qalbi keliyaan leeyahay oo ii ma qaybsamo e
2 Isna meel keli yah buu qabsaday, qamar-La-mood-yeey

IX

1 Anigaan dhiman, dhaanta deyn maayo e
2 Ilaahow iga dhaaf wachaan dhimo

X

1 Oh bottles, pour out your medicines,
2 And when you have emptied, resound with a love-song.

XI

1 If a potion tastes bitter,
2 And yet brings relief, would you give it up?

XII

1 Oh doctor, I have a pain in my heart,
2 Give me treatment, but don't put me in hospital!

28. *Independence*

ANONYMOUS

This song celebrates the unification of the former British Somaliland Protectorate with ex-Italian Somalia, the creation of the independent Somali Republic.

1 Freedom and dignity have reached us,
2 We have brought together the two lands.
3 Glory to God!
4 Say: 'It is God's victory[1],
5 It is God's victory!
6 We are victorious.'
7 Beat the song, join the dance!
8 Everyone, with all your might!
9 And now let us finish, cease!
10 It is God's victory!
11 It is God's victory!

[1] To understand the emotional appeal of this poem the reader should bear in mind that the expression 'God's victory' (Guul Alla) is the Somali equivalent of the Quranic *naṣru -llāhi* 'God's victory' or 'God's help'.

X

Quraaradayow, dawada quba
Oo qalfoofyohow, qaada dhaantada

XI

Hadday dawo Kuu qadhaadhdhahay
Oo dabiibi naftaada ma aad deyn?

XII

Aniga dhakhtaryohow, dhul baa i buka e
I dhaydhay, waadhka na ha i dhigin!

Gobannimo dhowaatay
Oo labadan is u geynay e
Waa gallada Ilaahii yoo
Dhaha guul Allee!
Guul Allee!
Waa guullaynay.
Garaaca ciyaarta!
Giddigiinna adkeeya!
Aan goynee, gam ka siiya!
Guul Allee!
Guul Allee!

C · RELIGIOUS POETRY IN ARABIC

29. *In Praise of Muḥammad Ṣaaliḥ*

MAḤAMMED ʿABDILLE ḤASAN

This hymn in praise of Muḥammad Ṣaaliḥ, founder of the Ṣaaliḥiya Brotherhood, is one of a number attributed to Maḥammed ʿAbdille Ḥasan and was apparently used by his followers as a war song in their holy war against the British, Italian, and Ethiopian administrations. It is still popular among the members of the Brotherhood.

1 Oh miraculous man of God,[1] Sheikh Muḥammad Ṣaaliḥ, the helper, Muḥammad Ṣaaliḥ,
2 Oh my teacher, my refuge, my stay, my reliance!
3 You are the epitome, and the essence of saints.
4 My goal, my defender, expounder of the prophets;
5 Magnet of knowledge, light of the pious;
6 (Guide of the) wandering pilgrims, oh loftiest canopy of heaven.
7 My heart is torn apart by longing, oh suns of the beloved.
8 You are my soul, my breath, oh most compassionate of the compassionate.
9 You are the seal of the faithful, the path of the caliphs.
10 You are the helper of mankind and djinns; come to my aid, never failing helper.
11 You are the patron of those who love God, oh prince of princes.
12 Oh protection of the ascendent, oh physician of physicians,
13 Our father, our father, oh helping hand of the poor;
14 Oh beloved Muḥammad, oh imam of the wise;
15 Oh my preserver, oh my guardian, oh doctor of doctors;
16 You are the feast of the learned; oh greatest of the great;
17 Oh secret of secrets, oh guardian of the generous.
18 Oh triumph of those who seek knowledge, come to us before our time is past;

[1] Lit. 'a thing for God', i.e. a person singled out by God and endowed with special grace (*karaama*) to pursue all the Muslim virtues and to perform miracles. Another interpretation is also put forward by some Somalis: '(Give me) a thing for (the sake of) God', i.e. 'Grant me a favour' or 'Answer my prayers'.

19 Seek pardon and forgiveness for us, and gather to you those who are far away.
20 Secure us from all evil, oh most steadfast of the steadfast.
21 My sighs are stilled, my tears are songs.
22 We complain of our distress, and you are the remedy for our weariness.
23 Oh my soul, my soul, source of the burning ardour which I endure;
24 With you is abundant grace, oh most generous of the generous.
25 Oh how I long for your riches, oh rejoicing's fulfilment!
26 The deceived one came to seek your riches, oh rectifier of the misled.
27 Oh say to the weariness of my ribs, 'I bring good news to the faithful followers'.
28 Blessing and peace be upon the best of the prophets,
29 And upon the family of the noble ones and the companions of the pious.

30. *The Evils of the Balwo*

MAḤAMMED ḤASAN

This poem, composed by a pious Somali Sheikh, is an attack upon the modern love-song (*balwo* or *heello*) of the towns. The word *balwo* is an Arabic loan word meaning originally 'calamity' or 'misfortune'. In the poem the sheikh takes the original sense of the word for granted and implies that this type of contemporary popular Somali song is well named. For these songs, of which examples will be found at pages 146–8, are considered by many of the more orthodox and conservative religious leaders to be degenerate and scandalous in the extreme. The immediate circumstances which gave rise to this tirade against *balwo* were that the author lived above a room in which young men regularly gathered to sing these love-songs. By day the sheikh's devotions were disturbed by the constant stream of irreligious noise, and by night sleep was impossible.

1 Oh my God, my God, have mercy on us and save us from the *balwo*.
2 The monarchs of old reigned and built their palaces,
3 But they fell short of achievement; they did not sojourn long in them and their desires were not fulfilled.
4 Now they lie prostrate where they struggled; they might well have never been.

5 Neither they nor those who destroyed them gained lasting ease.
6 They are a witness to God's words: 'The leaders of the wicked (shall plot, but only against themselves);'[1]
7 They bartered their faith for the world and the transaction brought them no gain.
8 The evil *balwo* songs came, bringing corruption and spreading sin,
9 And God was displeased with those who wrought such wrongfulness.
10 They wasted their substance in frivolity and dissipation,
11 They gathered together in debauchery and hungered after what is prohibited.
12 Women who became like devils lured them astray,
13 As the holy tradition says: 'They are the snares of the devil.'
14 Turn away from them, pay no heed to them, and abandon their places of song.
15 Achieve instead the success and strength which God gives, the Builder of the Throne.
16 Flee from these vain things, forsake them; their possession brings no happiness;
17 Abandon them, and those who seek them. Unhappy is the place of song!
18 The steadfast in the faith turned aside and put no trust in these things of the world.
19 They were strangers in the world as the Prophet said.
20 Oh my God, my God, have mercy on your servants and pity us!
21 My Lord, my All, save me from the demons.
22 My God, our Creator, bless Him who pastures (the world),
23 The beloved of God, our Lord, the leader of all, the intercessor.
24 Blessing be upon His family, His companions, His followers, and upon His helpers,
25 As long as it is said that 'the leaders of the wicked (shall plot, but only against themselves)',
26 And as long as the turtle-dove warbles on the tree.

[1] This passage is obscure. Our tentative interpretation is based on the conjecture that it refers to line 123 of the sixth Sura of the Quran, which runs as follows: 'And likewise We have put in every village (or town) leaders of its wicked ones so that they may plot there; but they shall plot only against themselves, without knowing it.'

31. *Praise be to Sheikh Isaaq*

ʿABDULLAAHI ḤAASHI

This hymn was composed in praise of Sheikh Isḥaaq, whose name Somalis normally pronounces as *Isaaq*. He was the founding ancestor of the Isaaq clans, and the poem constantly refers to the Sheikh's noble birth, his descent from the Quraysh (The House of the Prophet), and his missionary enterprise in coming from Arabia to settle in Somaliland and found the Isaaq peoples. The poem brings out very clearly the intercessory role of the saint and the importance of pilgrimage to his holy shrine at Mait, which in the Arabic version is spelt *Mayr* and is pronounced by Somalis as *Mayḍ*. Traditionally Sheikh Isḥaaq's arrival from Arabia is placed in the thirteenth century A.D. The poem is typical of many composed in Arabic in honour of Somali sheikhs.

In the Name of God, the Compassionate, the Merciful.

1 God protect us from every evil and unbelief: by the sanctity of the light of the Religion, Isḥaaq, my support.
2 I begin my composition with the mention of God and his praise: and I thank him for every assistance and grace.
3 I call down blessing upon the Chosen One, the best Messenger, Muḥammad, sent among the best community.
4 I address my supplication through my Sheikh and my forefather, my stay: through him I ask for help against every anxiety and distress.
5 He is the Pivot (of the Saints) and the Helper (of the Age),[1] the son of Aḥmad, the God-fearer, the lamp of the people of God, the sheikh of Divine Guidance.
6 Oh solace of the eye, oh utmost desire: oh light of the land of God, oh bountiful.
7 Oh thou illustrious in glory whose excellence is famed in every quarter, oh light of mine eyes.
8 Oh pure of soul, oh rightly guided one, oh lord of the Prophet's descendants,[2] grant me favour;
9 Oh scion of the Chosen One, oh thou who art our helper, and our refuge, do not ever forget us.

[1] The expressions 'Pivot' (*quṭb*) and 'Helper' (*ghawth*) belong to the technical vocabulary of Islamic mysticism.

[2] The Prophet's descendants, i.e. the *Ashraaf*.

10 Noble and accomplished, modest and dignified, sultan of the People of God, radiance of the Divine Law,

11 Praise will never cease upon him who enlivens our souls (and also) upon the Tree of ʿAdnaan,[1] the elect lords.

12 Oh Lord, perfume his grave and bestow on us every moment his beautiful mysteries.

13 My address concerns the praise of my Sheikh and my guide: my utmost goal and my strongest proof;

14 He is gentle and has embraced all mankind with his guidance, like his forefather—the best of creation, my most praiseworthy provider.

15 Bountiful, pure, ascetic, kind: how much virtue, learning, and compassion there is in him!

16 Great saint, those who are envious of him died in their anger: through whose generosity my poverty and distress will depart.

17 By mention of the saint of God our life is made happy; through his admirable qualities every sickness has been healed.

18 Oh saint of God, oh son of Aḥmad, oh thou who art called Isḥaaq, take pity on my complaint.

19 Oh saint of God, truly I am thy lowly slave; my hope rests on thee for relief from my distress and anxiety.

20 Oh saint of God, I direct myself towards thee for thou art my recourse in both abundance and adversity.

21 Oh saint of God, I am thy descendant, do not abandon me in terror.

22 Oh saint of God, truly I am thy postulant who has taken refuge in thee from the evil of this wretchedness.

23 Oh saint of God, I come to thee as a guest, succour me with thy approval and grace;

24 Oh saint of God, I have come to thee as a pilgrim, be my intercessor before the Lord of Creation.

25 Oh saint of God, oh son of Aḥmad, oh thou who art called Isḥaaq, take pity on my complaint.

26 Oh thou dweller on the sand-dunes of Mait,[2] the light of whose tomb has illumined the Yemen,

[1] ʿAdnaan, the ancestor of the Quraysh, the lineage to which the Prophet belonged.

[2] Mait, the place where Sheikh Isaaq's domed tomb lies, is an ancient centre of habitation on the Gulf of Aden coast in the Erigavo District of the Northern Region of the Somali Republic.

27 Help me, protect me, for my life has wasted away in vain; take me by thy hand, truly I have been ignorant through my misery.
28 Oh Lord, perfume his grave and bestow on us every moment his beautiful mysteries.
29 Our patron[1] came over the sea on a prayer-rug continuing until he reached a strange land.
30 He dwelt in it, and it was illuminated by his light: may the Lord of Creation requite him for his goodness.
31 Descendants without limit, numberless, spread abroad through him, men of rank,
32 Who have provided men of learning, saints, and spiritual leaders, whose noble lives belong to the heritage of the people.
33 I have set forth his qualities, oh my soul preserve thou the love of the physician of the heart, Isḥaaq, my reliance.
34 Assuredly he has embraced the dignity of both worlds, make his description the most glorious and the most exhalted.
35 Never did he depart from the rules of the Divine Law: Oh that my desires might be fulfilled through visiting him.
36 The Lord of the Throne has given him virtue and rank; upon him God's satisfaction dwells every hour.
37 Oh Lord, perfume his grave and bestow on us every moment his beautiful mysteries.
38 My true friend, is there anywhere the like of our spiritual leader; his foot is set in the presence of holiness, and so may it be strengthened.
39 He has been given grace from the God of the Worlds, and a rank which surpasses every rank.
40 My ardour increases as I mention him: may my soul and my whole being be a ransom for his goodness.
41 His miracles are like the sea, oh my friend, take refuge in him for thus thou wilt escape every evil and punishment.
42 Oh Lord, perfume his grave and bestow on us every moment his beautiful mysteries.
43 He is the noble leader from whose posterity my youth (comes): people of Paradise, nobles of the community.

[1] The term *quṭb* is translated here as 'patron'.

44 Oh People of the House of the Chosen One, you have attained the heights; upon you the people of the seven climes place their hopes.

45 Those who have loved you, oh People of the House of Muḥammad, have triumphed in this world and at the day of resurrection;

46 Love of you is food for the people of the mysteries, and mention of you lays bare every misfortune.

47 Success and prosperity be to those who feed upon your love; and woe unto those who hate you, my beloved ones.

48 May long life and its enjoyment remain in your protection; may peace be upon you, oh people of my love!

49 You are my loved ones and the support upon which I rely. By God! Be generous to me with every kind of favour.

50 You are the desire of my heart and the comfort of my body; you are the end of my striving, my soul, and my solace.

51 Oh Lord, perfume his grave and bestow on us every moment his beautiful mysteries.

52 My friend help me to weep, for truly love of them is my guide, my help, and my faith.

53 If fellowship and union with the loved ones, and visitation of the tomb of our ancestor, Isḥaaq, my support, have escaped me,

54 Then let me die full of longing, sadness, and regret, for I am foolish and forgetful of his house.

55 But I have not chosen any other in place of their love, and my separation was not according to my will.

56 How sorry I shall be if I do not see their resting places and their flags before death comes upon me.

57 I wonder whether time will bring us together, for my longing for them is my resting place and my desire.

58 Will those past nights return and will the victim of love then return?

59 Will those days which have passed amongst those old buildings

60 Return to us so that our eyes may be solaced by the showers of grace as long as doves coo?

61 When, oh people of Mait, will mine eyes behold you and my heart throb to the reunion and good tidings?

62 Oh Lord, perfume his grave and bestow on us every moment his beautiful mysteries.

63 Oh how my heart (is filled with longing) whenever (I hear) a youth saying: Oh my masters grant me the favour of visiting you (just once)!

64 Oh how my eyes (are filled with tears) whenever a whistling bird wails on a branch, or doves coo at dawn!

65 Through him I yearn with love for the worthy sayyids and with longing for those noble tombs.

66 May God water the grave in which our Imam is laid with showers of grace as long as doves coo.

67 Oh glances of God, oh His mercies; Oh breaths of God, visit my best treasure.

68 Bestow thy favour upon all those who are buried in the midst of Mait: grant them, my God, satisfaction and peace.

69 They are the light of mine eyes, manifest wherever they journeyed: Oh God, save me through them from disappointment;

70 Likewise, oh Lord, save me from unseen evil, from the evil of Satan, and from the evil of djinns;

71 My God, through Thy favour, forgive our sins: enlarge for us our life's necessities, and accept my entreaty;

72 Smooth out our needs and destroy our enemies, through the son of Aḥmad, for he is the sea of truth.

73 Through him and through the 'Power of Humanity', ʿAbdul Qaadir,[1] and through Al-ʿAydaruus of Aden,[2] grant us Paradise.

74 We have prayed to you, oh my Lord, through their authority and sanctity, to put to flight every distress.

75 Save us quickly by removing our troubles, life's straitened circumstances, the constriction of the grave and its suffocation;

76 Cover up our corruptions and heal our diseases through 'the father of young lions', Isḥaaq, my support.

77 Blessing and peace be at every moment upon Aḥmad Al-ʿAdnaan, 'he of the mole',[3]

[1] The founder of the Qaadiriya Sufi Order, to which the poet belongs. Sayyid ʿAbdul Qaadir al-Jiilaani died in Baghdad in A.D. 1166.

[2] One of the main Qaadiriya saints of Aden who died in A.D. 1503.

[3] A mole, i.e. a mark on the skin, here symbolizes 'the dark spot' or 'centre' in mystic experience.

78 Likewise upon the Family and the Companions of the Prophet, as long as lightning flashes and the turtle-dove warbles on a tree.

79 And upon the Sheikh of Sheikhs, the son of Aḥmad, the man of piety, and upon the sons of the Sayyids, the people of sanctity.

ORIGINAL ARABIC TEXTS

29. *In Praise of Muḥammad Ṣaalih*

Lines 1–29

شيء لله شيخ محمد صالح — المدد يا محمد صالح
يا استاذي وملاذي — وعمادي واعتمادي
ومعيني ومعني — ومعاني الاولياء
ومصيري ونصيري — ومبين الانبياء
ومقنا طيس العلوم — ومنير الاتقياء
وسيا حين الأراضي — يا سماء أعلا السماء
شق قلبي لاشتياق — يا شموسي الاحباء
أنت روحي وراحي — ورحيم الرحماء
انت ختم الحنفاء — يا خليف الخلفاء
أنت غوث الثقلين — إغث يا غوث الورى
يا اساس الأوداء — يا أمير الامراء
يا طلا أهل الطلوع — يا طبيب الاطباء
يا أبانا يا أبانا — يا أسيد الفقراء
يا حبيبي يا كبير — يا إمام الاذكياء
يا حفيظي يا حبيبي — يا حكيم الحكماء
أنت عيد العلماء — يا عظيم العظماء
يا كمين الكميا — يا كفيل الكرماء
يا فتوح العارفين — أدركنا قبل الفناء
جد لعفو وغفران — وأقرب من عندك نار
إمنا عن كل سوء — يا أمين الامناء
وأنفاسي ساعات — ودموعي كالغناء
واشتكينا بضناء — والدواء فيك مناء
وفؤادي يا فؤادي — أجلة من حر المرضاء
ولك الفضل الجزيل — يا كريم الكرماء
كم اب جو منك غناء — يا ذمام بالهناء
ماد غاوي لغنا لكم — يا رشيد الأغوياء
وقل طلع الطلع الضلوع — ابشر ببشر الولاء
وصلاة ثم وسلام — على خير الانبياء
وعلى آل الكرام — واصحاب الاتقياء

30. *The Evils of the Balwo*

Lines 1–26

الهي يا الهي أرحم　　وسلمنا منه البلوى
ملوك الدهر قد سادوا　　وشادوا في مبانيها
وما وصلوا وما قطعوا　　وما نالوا منا ليها
فكم حرس مصاريهم　　وما كادوا يملكونها
فما طابت ولا طابت　　لقا ضيها وبانيها
فقول الله قد شهدوا　　فسجروها أكابرها
فما لهوا الدين بالدنيا　　فما رجعت تجارتها
فبلواه لقد ظهرت　　بأفواه فشوها فيها
لقد بين الله على　　رجال قد يعفا فيها
فما خوا الحال في لهو　　ولعبا في مخاريها
لفياهم قد اجتمعوا　　تقلدوا في مناهيها
فأمراهم وأخواهم　　نساء قد تشبطها
لقد وردت أحاديث　　حبائل للنسا فيها
قد نسه ولا تفعل بها　　واتزيت مغانيها
تنفل لمرة وفوته　　منه الله العرسه بانيها
فأهجرها وجاهدها　　فما تغن حمايتها
وحل عنا وسائلها　　فما أتقى مغانيها
هدايات الدين قد ناهوا　　وناقة لمه أمانيها
فكم غدباد في الدنيا　　كما قد قال مرسلها
الحمد الحمد أرحم　　ببعد قد هنى فيها
يا رب وحسب　　أمرنا منه خفائلها
وصلى الله بارئنا　　على منه كانه يرعاها
حبيب الله سيدنا　　أمام الكل شافعها
وآل ثم أصحاب　　واتباع وواليها
متى ما قال قائلها　　فسجرها أكابرها
وما قد عود العشرى　　مع الأشبار شا معها

31. *Praise be to Sheikh Isaaq*

Lines 1–14

بسم الله الرحمن الرحيم

إلهي أجرنا من كل شر وفتنة ... بحرمة نور الله بن إسحاق عمدتي

بدأت بذكر الله نظمي وحمده ... وأشكره من كل نصر ونعمة

وصليت بالمختار أفضل مرسل ... محمد المبعوث من خير أمة

توسلت بشيخي وجدي وعمدتي ... به أستغيث كل كرب وشدة

هو القطب والغوث ابن أحمد ذو التقى ... وقنديل أهل الله شيخ الهداية

ألا يا قرير العين يا غاية المنى ... ويا نور أرض الله يا ذا العطية

ألا يا شهير الفخر من شاع فضله ... على سائر الأقطار يا نور مقلتي

ألا يا زكي النفس يا ذا الهداية ... ويا سيد الأشراف جد لي بنفحة

ألا يا سليل المصطفى يا غياثنا ... وموئلنا لا تنسنا قد تجلي

شريف ظريف ذو حياء وهيبة ... وسلطان أهل الله شمس الشريعة

فلا تنقضي أمداح محيي نفوسنا ... إلى دوحة العدنان سادات صفوة

فيا رب عطر قبره وأمدنا ... بأسرار الحسناء في كل لحظة

أحيد تكلم عن مدح شيخي ومرشدي ... وغاية مقصودي وأعظم حجتي

فلم يبق وكن عم الأنام برشده ... كجده خير الخلق أحمد عدتي

Lines 15–31

سخي زكي زاهد متعطف   فكم فيه من فضل وعلم ورحمة
ولي عظيم مات غيظا حسوده   جواد به تذهب فقري وفاقتي
بنا لولي الله قد طاب عيشنا   بأوصافه الحسنى شفا كل علة
الا يا ولي الله يا ابن احمد   ويا من سما اسحاق ارحم شكايتي
الا يا ولي الله اني عبيدكم   فمنكم ارجي كشف ضري وكربتي
الا يا ولي الله اني قصدتكم   فانتم رجوعي في رخائي وشدتي
الا يا ولي الله اني حفيدكم   فلا تتركوني في الامور الفزيعة
الا يا ولي الله اني مريدكم   فلله ت البيلم ستر هذي الدنيئة
الا يا ولي الله اني دخيلكم   فمنوا اغياثي بالرضا والكرامة
الا يا ولي الله جئتك زائرا   فمن لي شفيعا عند رب البرية
الا يا ولي الله يا ابن احمد   ويا من سمي اسحاق ارحم شكايتي
ايا من سكن كشبان مع وقته   اللتي ضوؤها قد نار ارض اليمانة
اغثني اجرني ضاع عمري باطلا   وخذ بيدي اني جهلت بشقوة
فيا رب عطر قبره وامدنا   باسرار الحسناء في كل لحظة
مشى قطبنا في اليم فوق سجادة   وما زال حتى جاء في ارض غربة
فسكن فيها واستنار بنوره   فيا حسنه جازاه رب البرية
وفاضت به ذرية ليس تحصر   تحصر ولا عد وهم اهل رفعة

Lines 32–48

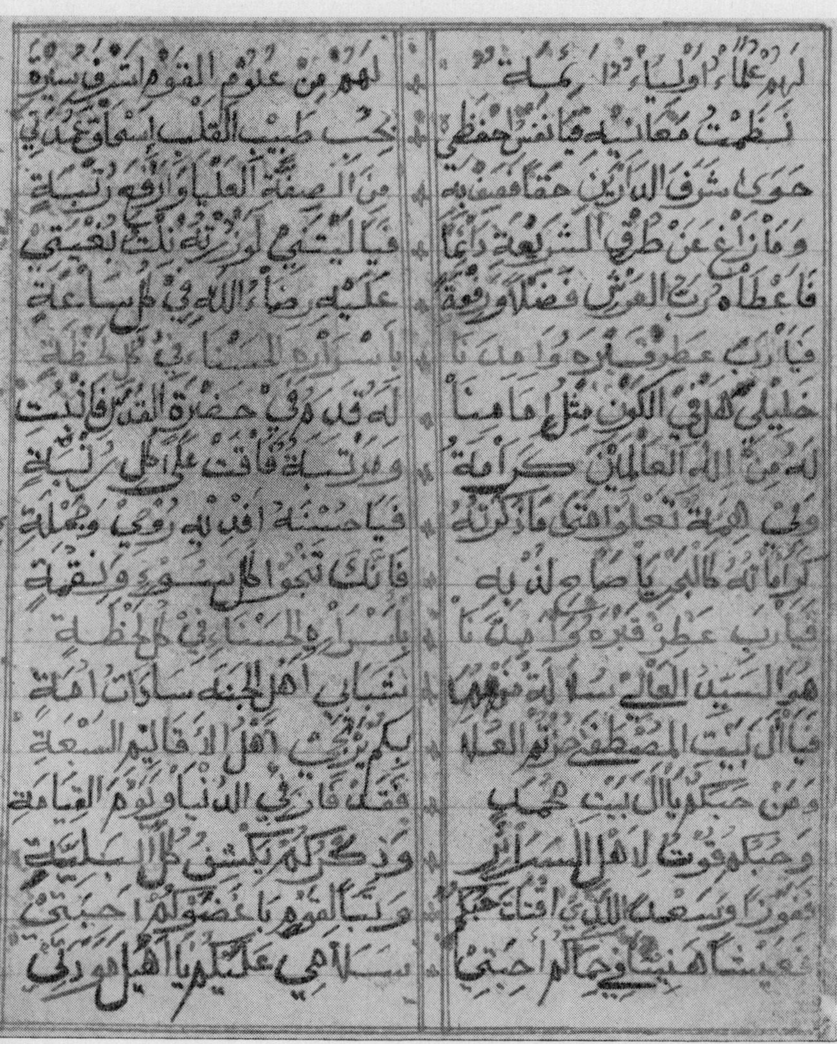

Lines 49–65

فانتم احبابي وعروة موثقي　　فبالله جودوا لي بالوان نعمة

وانتم منا قلبي وراحة قالبي　　وانتم مرادي بل وروحي وراحتي

فيا رب عطر قبره وامددنا　　باسراره الحسنا في كل لحظة

خليلي اعني بالبكاء فانني　　ارى جبهم رشدي وعوني وهمتي

اذا فاتني قرب الاحبة واللقا　　وزورة قبر الحب اسحاق عمدتي

فدعني امت شوقا وحزنا وحسرة　　فاني غبي غافل عن اهلتي

ولكنني ما اخترت شيئا لحبهم　　ولا فرقتي عنهم كلم ارادتي

فوا اسفي ان لم ارى عن ربوعهم　　واعلامهم من قبل اتاتي منيتي

ترى يجمع الايام بيني وبينهم　　فشوقي اليهم مقعد وصبابتي

فهل لليالي الماضيات بعودة　　وهل لقتيل الحب اذن برجعة

وعل لايام اللتي قد تصارمت　　على بين هاتيك القصور القديمة

تعود لنا حتى تقر عيوننا　　بوابل رحمات من الورق غنت

متى يا اهيل الميرغني تراكم　　ويهتز قلبي باللقا والبشارة

فيا رب عطر قبره وامددنا　　باسراره الحسنا في كل لحظة

الا ما لقلبي كل ما قال ذو صبا　　ايا ساداتي منوا علي بزورة

الا ما لمهيشفي كلما ناح صافر　　على الغصن او سجع الحمام سحيرة

اجن له وحب الى خير سادة　　وشوقا الى تلك القباب الكريمة

Lines 66–79

سقى الله قبرا حل فيه امامنا   بوابل رحمات مدى الورق غنت

فيا نفحات الله يا رحماته   ويا نفحات الله زر خير ذخرتي

وعمم لاصحاب ثوو وسط مرة   حباهم الهي بالرضا والسلامة

فهم نور عيني ظاهرا وسرا   بهم نجني يا رب من عين خيبة

كذا نجني يا رب من شر غيبة   ومن شر شيطان ومن شر جنة

الهي بفضل منك فاغفر ذنوبنا   ووسع لنا الارزاق واقبل وسيلتي

وسهل لنا الحاجات واهلك عداتنا   بجاه ابن احمد فهو نجم الحقيقة

به وبسلطان الورى عبد القادر   وبالعيدروس العيني جد جنة

سألناك يا ربي اليك بجاههم   وحرمتهم تكشف كل البلية

اجرنا سريعا بانجلاء كروبنا   وتضييق عيش ضغط قبر وركبة

واستر لنا العورات واشف سقامنا   بجاه ابي الاشبال اسحاق عمدتي

وصل وسلم كل وقت وساعة   على احمد العدنان صاحب شفاعة

كذا الآل والاصحاب ما لاح بارق   وما غردت قمرية فوق دوحة

وشيخ الشيوخ جل احمد ذو التقى   واولاده السادات اهل الولاية

PRINTED IN GREAT BRITAIN
AT THE UNIVERSITY PRESS, OXFORD
BY VIVIAN RIDLER
PRINTER TO THE UNIVERSITY